FIFTEENTH EDITION

STUDY GUIDE FOR MODERN Real Estate Practice

Fillmore W. Galaty · Wellington J. Allaway · Robert C. Kyle

Dearborn™
Real Estate Education

Vice President: Carol L. Luitjens
Executive Editor: Diana Faulhaber
Senior Development Editor: Louise Benzer
Art and Design Manager: Lucy Jenkins
Typography and Graphics: Bill Magargal
Managing Editor: Ronald J. Liszkowski

Published by Real Estate Education Company®
a Kaplan Professional Company®
155 North Wacker Drive
Chicago, IL 60606-1719
(312) 836-4400
http://www.dearborn.com

Printed in the United States of America.

02 10 9 8 7 6

Contents

Preface

Most students find their real estate principles class to be a challenging, rewarding and traumatic experience, all at the same time. For some, mastering the basic jargon of the real estate industry can be as demanding as learning a foreign language. Students who have not attended classes or studied for exams for several years sometimes find it difficult to get back into the habit—particularly when they have other important demands on their time, and homework is just another responsibility among many. Real Estate Education Company® is aware of the particular challenges that face today's real estate students. This ***Study Guide for Modern Real Estate Practice*** was written with your needs in mind.

About This Book

This *Study Guide* is designed to be used in conjunction with *Modern Real Estate Practice*, 15th Edition, by Galaty, Allaway and Kyle. It can also be used with the various state supplements, including the state "Practice & Law" series. Each chapter in the *Study Guide* corresponds to a chapter in the main text.

The *Study Guide* is intended to reinforce and elaborate on the basic information provided in *Modern Real Estate Practice.* Specifically, it is designed to help you master the three fundamental goals that are vital to academic success:

1. **recognize** important terms and concepts;
2. **evaluate** your understanding of basic real estate issues; and
3. **apply** learned principles to real-world practice.

The preceding goals form the basis for the basic **learning objectives** of the *Study Guide for Modern Real Estate Practice:*

- **define and explain** fundamental concepts and vocabulary terms of the real estate industry;
- **identify and discuss** the characteristics of various legal and financial relationships; and
- **perform and apply** basic financial and property-related calculations.

To help you along the way, this *Study Guide* uses several different learning strategies: an approach called **multitesting**. Each of the styles of self-testing included here has been proven effective in helping students not only to memorize factual information, but actually to retain the material in a constructive way. By working through the various components of each chapter, you will be reinforcing your real estate knowledge as well as your test-taking skills.

Why a Multitesting Approach?

The advantage of the multitesting approach is that the same material is tested repeatedly, but in different styles. While the real estate examination itself is exclusively multiple-choice, the use of other testing styles helps reinforce your understanding of the subject matter. The stronger your basic understanding of basic terms and concepts, the more prepared you'll be for possible exam curveballs.

> **Note!** This *Study Guide* is NOT a substitute for attending class or reading the main text! Rather, it is a tool to help you understand and retain what you've learned and read.

Before You Start . . .

This Preface includes complete instructions for all the exercises contained in the *Study Guide*. You may refer to these instructions at any time as you work through the various problem sections of each chapter. In addition, the instructions include **Study Strategies**: tips and tools you can use to make the *Study Guide* exercises as effective as possible.

Acknowledgements

The following individuals provided invaluable professional guidance and real-world expertise in the development of this *Study Guide*:

Donna Lee Higgins, O'Conor, Piper & Flynn/ERA Training

Emily M. Mintz, Long & Foster Institute of Real Estate

Colin F. McGowan, Director, Frederick Academy of Real Estate

Walt McLaughlin, McColly School of Real Estate

Instructions

How To Use the *Study Guide*

Each chapter in this *Study Guide* includes the following sections:

Flash Cards

There is no substitute for memorizing a new vocabulary. Without the basic vocabulary, there is no way to answer true or false questions, multiple-choice questions or a consumer's question.

STUDY STRATEGY: *Each flash card page is perforated. After removing it from the book, cut the individual cards apart using scissors. Carry the cards with you and, whenever possible, review them. When you are consistently accurate, remove that card and concentrate on the remaining terms that are eluding you. Learning these basic definitions leads to the next study guide, matching.*

Key Term Matching

Test yourself to see how many of the key terms and other important real estate words you can match with their correct definitions. In some chapters, we've split this section into two parts to make it easier for you to use. Each part is completely self-contained. Simply write the key term in the blank next to the definition.

STUDY STRATEGY: *First fill in the blanks and check your answers. Then, later, you can also use this section for* more *study by covering the answer you have written in and verbally (or mentally) give the definition, or cover the definition and pronounce the term. Both exercises will reinforce your basic knowledge of key definitions.*

True or False

This section helps prepare you for the multiple-choice questions used on most exams. You are presented with a series of statements based on material in the main text. Determine whether the statement is true or false, and circle the **T** or **F** accordingly.

STUDY STRATEGY: *Be careful! These statements are designed to test how closely you can read, and how clearly you understand what you've read: they may be tricky. There may be only one word that makes the entire statement false. The answer key provides explanations for all the questions with False as the answer.*

Here's an example:

14. T F A real estate appraiser is licensed by the state to buy, sell, rent or lease real property.

*The statement is clearly **False**. Circle the **F**. In the Answer Key, you would find:*

14. False A real estate broker is licensed by the state to buy, sell, rent or lease real property.

The focus of the preceding question is clearly on the *characteristics of a real estate broker*, not what an appraiser can do. The better choice is to stick to the question's main idea. As a rule, the smaller the changes you have to make to create a true statement, the better. In this example, changing only one word (appraiser to broker) makes the statement true.

Multiple-choice Review

Each chapter of the main text includes a section of multiple-choice questions. It may help to recognize that each multiple-choice question is actually four true or false statements. The question formats used in the *Study Guide* help you retain information as well as prepare for the format and structure of the licensing exam.

STUDY STRATEGY: *Most multiple-choice questions will consist of three false statements (answers) and one true statement. Circle the letter of the answer that makes a true ending to the question. For study purposes (and rarely on official exams), we ask you to compile a list of information. These questions consist of three true statements and one false answer. These are characterized by these words... "All of the following are true ... EXCEPT..." In this situation, you choose the exception to the list.*

Illustrations

Many people remember information through pictures. In these sections, you are asked to complete an illustration of one or more basic concepts. Some of the illustrations are reproduced from the main text, while most have been created especially for this *Study Guide*. Some illustrations ask you simply to label certain elements; for others, you may need to analyze information and fill in a practice-related form.

STUDY STRATEGY: *Try to visualize the concepts presented in the illustrations. Creating a useful mental picture may be very helpful to recall during the exam.*

Logic Problems

When working on a complicated fact-pattern problem (whether in this *Study Guide* or on the real estate licensing examination), draw a picture. Make a chart or diagram of the transactions involved in the problem. Label each actor by identifier and illustrate the role he or she plays in the event. For instance, if the problem is "F conveyed Blueacres to G, who conveyed a life estate pur autre vie to H, measured by the life of Y, retaining a reversionary interest," you might draw a diagram like this:

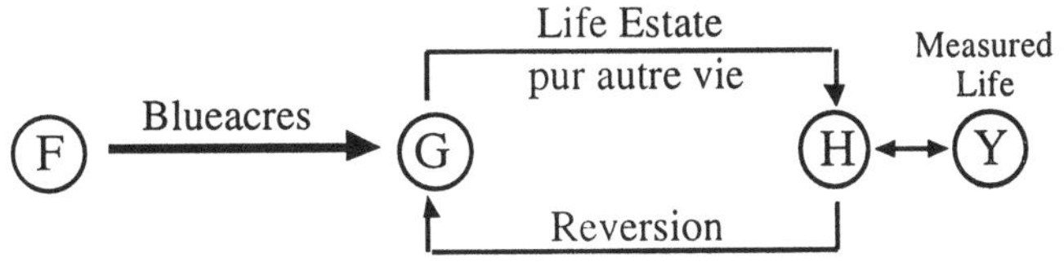

Math Problems

When you're faced with a math problem, read the whole question carefully! Sometimes testers (and even this *Study Guide*) will include distracting or irrelevant facts or numbers, to make sure you know not only how to perform certain calculations, but know what information you need to do it. For example, if a question wants you to calculate a broker's commission on a sale, you can disregard information about the asking price or mortgage.

Never assume! You should be able to answer a question based only on the facts you're given. Be sure to pay attention to what you're really being asked to do. Don't make the mistake of trying to rewrite the question instead of choosing the correct answer to the given question.

Answer Key

The *Study Guide* includes a complete set of answers at the end of each chapter so that you can assess your comprehension before proceding to the next chapter.

Don't look at the answers until you've completed all the sections in the chapter! If you check your answers after each section, you might accidentally peek at the correct responses for the next section. While that might improve your overall scores in the *Study Guide*, it won't help your score where it counts ... on the licensing exam.

Final Hints

Write in this book! • *Tear out the flash cards and USE them.*

This isn't a leather-bound masterpiece destined for your library. It is a hands-on, practical guide to help you study for your modern real estate practice.

Math *Quick-Review*

Looking for a quick review of some real estate math principles? Use the following chart to locate the questions in this *Study Guide* that ask you to perform real estate math calculations. The page reference given is for the chapter's first math question. While this book is not intended to offer a thorough math review, working through the math questions will help you focus on problem areas for further study.

TOPIC	CHAPTER	QUESTIONS	PAGE
ad valorem taxes	10	3, 13	76
appraisal	18	1, 9, 12, 14	144
capital gains, equity	3	4, 6	17
commercial leases	16	Figure 16.1	133
commissions *(calculating percentages)*	6	1, 2, 3, 4, 5	41
commissions, rent per square unit	17	4, 5	137
commissions *(calculating compensation)*	5	1, 2, 3, 4, 5	33
cost per square unit, calculating size	9	1, 2, 3, 9	67
equity	3	12	18
estate taxes	12	14	94
homestead exemptions	7	10	52
mortgage types, payments, P&I	15	Figure 15.1, 15.2, also 11, 14, 15, 16, 18	121
PITI	3	9, 11	17
points, percentages, foreclosure	14	4, 9, 13, 15	109
proration, credit/debit	22	1 - 5	179
sales contract calculations	11	Figure 11.1	87
sample settlement statement	22	Figure 22.1	180
transfer tax	12	15, 18	94

Introduction to the Real Estate Industry

1

Matching

Write the matching term on the appropriate line.

- home inspection
- salesperson
- appraisal
- market
- brokerage
- demand
- REALTOR®
- supply
- broker
- property management

1. ________________ A place where goods can be bought and sold and a price for goods established
2. ________________ The amount of goods available in the market to be sold at a given price
3. ________________ Person who performs real estate activities while employed by or associated with a licensed real estate broker
4. ________________ In real estate, licensed person who acts as an intermediary on behalf of others for a fee or commission
5. ________________ Maintaining and administering another's property for a fee
6. ________________ Process of using established methods and good judgment to estimate the value of a property
7. ________________ The bringing together of parties interested in making a real estate transaction
8. ________________ The amount of goods people are willing and able to buy at a given price
9. ________________ Report based on visual survey of property structure, systems and site conditions
10. ________________ Adheres to NAR's Code of Ethics

True or False

Circle the answer

1. T F The five classes of real estate mentioned in the main text are residential, commercial, rental, agricultural and special purpose.
2. T F The real estate market is generally slow to adjust to the changing forces of supply and demand.
3. T F The supply of labor and the cost of construction generally have a direct effect on the demand for real estate in a market.
4. T F Real estate agents generally tend to specialize in one activity or class of real estate.
5. T F Warehouses, factories and power plants are examples of commercial property.
6. T F Members of the National Association of Real Estate Brokers are known as REALTORS®

True or False (Continued)

7. T F In general, the most widely recognized real estate activity is brokerage.

8. T F Finding funds to put together real estate transactions is called appraising.

9. T F Real estate activity is relatively slow to adjust to the force of supply and demand.

10. T F The rental market is characterized by space used temporarily by lease.

Multiple Choice

Circle A, B, C or D

1. Office buildings and retail space are examples of
   A. commercial real estate.
   B. special-use real estate.
   C. residential property.
   D. properties that involve a tenant-landlord relationship.

2. A person who advises a real estate client who is making a purchase to use or invest in real estate is called a(n)
   A. educator.
   B. mortgage broker.
   C. counselor.
   D. subdivider.

3. All of the following factors will tend to affect demand EXCEPT
   A. labor costs.
   B. employment levels.
   C. wage rates.
   D. demographics.

4. The population of a town suddenly increases. Which of the following is most likely to occur?
   A. Rental rates fall due to increased competition.
   B. Demand for housing decreases.
   C. New housing starts will decrease.
   D. Real estate prices will increase.

5. Property management, appraisal, financing and development are all
   A. specializations directly linked to state and federal government financial policies.
   B. separate professions within the real estate industry.
   C. real estate brokerage professions.
   D. demographic factors that affect demand for real property in a commercial market.

6. The idea that no two parcels of land are exactly alike is called
   A. immobility.
   B. subdivision.
   C. uniqueness.
   D. location.

7. All of the following factors can affect the supply of real estate EXCEPT
   A. demographics.
   B. labor force.
   C. construction costs.
   D. government controls.

8. A property owner who does not want to deal with the everyday tasks of managing a rental property can hire a(n)
   A. property manager.
   B. appraiser.
   C. home inspector.
   D. developer.

9. In general, when the supply of a certain commodity decreases while demand remains the same, the price of that commodity will do which of the following?
   A. Tend to remain the same
   B. Tend to increase
   C. Decrease
   D. Price will not be affected.

10. All of the following are examples of government policies that can affect the real estate market EXCEPT
    A. Federal Reserve Board's discount rate.
    B. shortage of skilled labor or building materials.
    C. land-use controls such as zoning.
    D. federal environmental regulations.

Flash Cards (Pull out page & cut with scissors)

property management	**brokerage**
REALTOR®	**categories of real property**
real property	**demand**
salesperson	**development**
subdivision	**market**
supply	**National Association of Real Estate Brokers (NAREB)**

Bringing together parties interested in a real estate transaction

Chapter 1

Management of another's property for compensation

Chapter 1

Residential, Commercial, Industrial, Agricultural, Special Purpose

Chapter 1

Member of National Association of REALTORS®, adhere to Code of Ethics

Chapter 1

Amount of goods people are willing and able to buy

Chapter 1

Interests, benefits and rights associated with real estate ownership

Chapter 1

Construction of improvements on land, i.e., new homes, water lines

Chapter 1

Performs real estate activities under supervision of licensed real estate broker

Chapter 1

Place where goods are bought and sold, price is established

Chapter 1

Splitting a single property into smaller parcels

Chapter 1

Dedicated to equal housing opportunity, members are REALTISTS

Chapter 1

Amount of goods available in the market to be sold at a given price

Chapter 1

Answer Key

KEY TERM MATCHING

1. market
2. supply
3. salesperson
4. broker
5. property management
6. appraisal
7. brokerage
8. demand
9. home inspection
10. REALTOR®

TRUE OR FALSE

1. False The five classes of real estate mentioned in the text are residential, commercial, industrial, agricultural and special-purpose.
2. True
3. False Supply of labor and the cost of construction generally have a direct effect on the supply of real estate in a market.
4. True
5. False Warehouses, factories and power plants are examples of industrial property.
6. False Members of the National Association of Real Estate Brokers are known as Realtists. REALTORS® are members of the National Association of REALTORS®.
7. True
8. False Finding funds involves financing; appraising is estimating the value of property.
9. True
10. True

MULTIPLE CHOICE

1. A Special use includes churches and dormitories; not all office and retail space involves leases.
2. C An educator provides education, a mortgage broker searches for financing, and a subdivider splits larger properties into smaller ones.
3. A Labor costs affect the supply; another factor affecting demand is population.
4. D Rental rates would increase, demand for housing will increase, and more new homes will be started to satisfy demand.
5. B These are not linked to the government, and they are not all linked to real estate brokerage.
6. C Another word for uniqueness is nonhomogeneity.
7. A Demographics affects the demand for real estate.
8. A An appraiser estimates value, a home inspector looks for problems with the property and the developer improves the property.
9. B When consumers continue to demand a product, and there isn't enough to go around, the price generally increases.
10. B A shortage of skilled labor will affect the supply of real estate, and this is not generally associated with government policies.

2

Real Property and the Law

Matching

Write the matching term on the appropriate line.

- annexation ✓
- bundle of legal rights ✓
- improvement ✓
- surface rights
- emblements ✓
- fixture ✓
- subsurface rights ✓
- real estate ✓
- real property ✓
- severance ✓
- personal property ✓
- water rights ✓
- chattels ✓
- trade fixture ✓
- air rights ✓

1. trade fixtures An article installed by a tenant under a commercial lease, removable before the lease expires
2. personal property Any property that is not real property
3. annexation Conversion of personal property to real property
4. bundle of legal rights Ownership of all legal rights to the land: control, possession, exclusion, enjoyment and disposition
5. real property The interests, benefits and rights of owning real estate
6. air rights The right to use the open space above the surface of a property
7. real estate A portion of the earth's surface extending down to the center and up into space, including all natural and artificial attachments
8. subsurface rights Ownership rights in the water, minerals, gas and oil that lie beneath a parcel of land
9. fixture Personal property that is converted to real property by being permanently attached to the realty
10. improvement Any structure or modification erected or imposed on a site to enhance the value of the property
11. severance Changing an item of real estate to personal property by detaching it from the land
12. surface rights Ownership rights excluding air or mineral rights
13. water rights Common law rights of owners of land next to rivers, lakes or oceans
14. ~~emblements~~ chattels Another name for personal property
15. ~~chattels~~ emblements Growing crops such as corn or soybeans that remain personal property

Flash Cards (Pull out page & cut with scissors)

annexation	improvement
appurtenance	personal property
bundle of legal rights	physical characteristics of real estate (3)
economic characteristics of real estate (4)	real property
emblements	severance
fixture	trade fixture

Man-made attachment to the land, such as a building, streets, utilities

Chapter 2

Change personal property to real property, such as mixing sand, stone and cement, and making a sidewalk

Chapter 2

Movable objects, not real property, sometimes called chattels, such as cars, cash, stock

Chapter 2

Right, privilege or improvement belonging to, and passing with the land

Chapter 2

Immobility, Indestructiblity, Uniqueness (nonhomogeneity)

Chapter 2

Ownership of all legal rights: control, possession, use, disposition, enjoyment

Chapter 2

Interests, benefits and rights inherent in real estate ownership.

Chapter 2

Scarcity, improvements, permanence of investment, area preference (location)

Chapter 2

Changing of real to personal property, such as cutting down a tree, removing stained glass window

Chapter 2

Annual, harvestable crops such as corn, wheat; personal property

Chapter 2

Personal property: Business item permanently attached by tenant. May be removed up to last day of lease. If left, landlord acquires by process of accession.

Chapter 2

Item that was once personal property and is now permanently affixed and is real property, such as a chandelier or ceiling fan

Chapter 2

Circle the answer — True or False

1. T F The terms "land, "real estate" and "real property" are interchangeable: they all refer to the same thing.
2. T F Real property is defined as the earth's surface extending downward to the center of the earth and upward to infinity, including permanent natural objects such as trees and water.
3. T F The term "real property" includes land, rights and real estate.
4. T F The transfer of the right to use the surface of the earth always includes the right to the natural resources that lie beneath the surface of the earth.
5. T F Trees, perennial shrubbery and grasses that do not require annual cultivation are considered personal property.
6. T F The process by which personal property becomes real property is referred to as "annexation."
7. T F A trade fixture is an article owned by a tenant and attached to a rented space or building used in conducting a business.
8. T F The economic characteristics of real estate are scarcity, improvements, permanence of investment and uniqueness.
9. T F Immobility, indestructibility and scarcity are physical characteristics of real property.
10. T F The image of a bundle of sticks is the traditional illustration of the set of legal rights of ownership.

Real Property or Personal Property?

Enter check marks in the appropriate columns to indicate whether each item is real or personal property, and whether it is a fixture or a trade fixture.

Property Description	Type of Property		Fixture	Trade Fixture
	Real	Personal		
1. Sidewalks and sewers in a subdivision				
2. Bushes surrounding a residence				
3. Wheat or corn crops on a farm				
4. Kitchen sink installed in a home				
5. Booths in a restaurant installed by a tenant				
6. Curtains installed by a tenant				
7. Pumps installed by a gas station tenant				
8. Machinery installed by landowner				
9. Crystal chandelier hung from the ceiling				
10. 80 gallon water heater with fiberglas insulating jacket				

Multiple Choice

Circle A, B, C or D

1. Land, mineral, and air rights in the land are included in the definition of
   A. attachments.
   B. real property.
   C. subsurface rights.
   D. improvements.

2. Which of the following is an example of an economic characteristic of land?
   A. Immobility
   B. Indestructibility
   C. Uniqueness
   D. Scarcity

3. Another word for uniqueness is
   A. scarcity.
   B. nonhomogeneity.
   C. fructus industriales.
   D. immobility.

4. All of the following are included in the bundle of rights EXCEPT
   A. possession.
   B. control.
   C. exclusion.
   D. expansion.

5. The right to control the use of the property and to dispose of it by will or deed are contained in the
   A. bundle of rights.
   B. deed.
   C. common law of real property.
   D. statutory law of the state.

6. Growing trees, fences and buildings would all be considered
   A. chattels.
   B. land.
   C. fixtures.
   D. real estate.

7. The most important economic characteristic of land is
   A. permanence.
   B. area preference.
   C. uniqueness.
   D. possession.

8. A tenant farmer built a chicken coop and a tool shed. These buildings belong to the
   A. tenant.
   B. owner of the real estate.
   C. owner but he must reimburse the tenant.
   D. tenant but he must pay additional rent for them.

9. The developer added sewer lines, utilities and built two streets. What are these items called?
   A. Fixtures
   B. Additions
   C. Improvements
   D. Permanence of Investment

10. The new owner received the land, the right to drive on his neighbor's driveway in addition to the house and garage. The right, the house, and garage are examples of
    A. improvements.
    B. fixtures.
    C. appurtenances.
    D. the bundle of rights.

11. Intent, method of annexation, adaptation and agreement are the legal tests for determining whether an item is
    A. a chattel or an emblement.
    B. real property or personal property.
    C. land or real estate.
    D. fructus naturales or industriales.

12. After suffering through a tornado and then flooding from the river, the buildings were gone. The land was still there. This is an example of
    A. uniqueness.
    B. scarcity.
    C. area preference.
    D. indestructibility.

13. The buyer asked the real estate agent to prepare several documents relating to the transfer of real property. Under these circumstances, the agent should
    A. ask the broker for assistance.
    B. draw up the documents.
    C. ignore the instructions.
    D. refer the buyer to an attorney.

Multiple Choice (Continued)

14. B particularly liked the ornate brass lighting fixtures in H's house, and immediately made an offer, which H accepted. On moving day, B discovered that H had replaced all the ornate brass fixtures with plain steel ones. Which of the following is most likely a correct assumption?
    A. H: "As long as I replaced them with something of comparable value, I can take them with me."
    B. B: "Lighting fixtures are normally considered to be real estate."
    C. H: "The lighting fixtures were personal property when I bought them at the store, so they're personal property forever."
    D. H: "The lighting fixtures belong to me because I installed them."

15. The farmer has posted a number of "No Trespassing" and "No Hunting" signs on the property. Which "stick" in the bundle of rights gives the farmer this authority?
    A. Exclusion
    B. Enjoyment
    C. Control
    D. Disposition

Answer Key

KEY TERM MATCHING

1. trade fixture
2. personal property
3. annexation
4. bundle of legal rights
5. real property
6. air rights
7. real estate
8. subsurface rights
9. fixture
10. improvements
11. severance
12. surface rights
13. water rights
14. chattels
15. emblements

TRUE OR FALSE

1. False — The terms "land," "real estate" and "real property" are not interchangeable: They refer to different aspects of the same thing.
2. False — Land is defined as the earth's surface extending downward to the center of the earth and upward to infinity, including permanent natural objects such as trees and water. Real property is defined as the interests, benefits and rights inherent in the ownership of real estate.
3. True
4. False — The transfer of the surface does not necessarily include the rights to the subsurface rights, the natural resources that lie beneath the surface.
5. False — Trees, perennial shrubbery and grasses that do not require annual cultivation are considered real property.
6. True
7. True
8. False — Economic characteristics of land include scarcity, improvements, permanence of investment and area preference.
9. False — Physical characteristics of land include immobility, indestructibility and uniqueness.
10. True

Answer Key (Continued)

MULTIPLE CHOICE

1. B Subsurface rights and improvements are included in the definition of real estate. Real property also includes rights and privileges.

2. D A, B and C are physical characteristics.

3. B Uniqueness, or nonhomogeneity, both indicate that no two parcels of land are alike.

4. D The bundle of rights includes possession, control, exclusion, but not the right to expand.

5. A Real property is described as a bundle of legal rights.

6. D The definition of real estate includes growing trees, fences and buildings. Chattels are personal property. Definition of land would not include fences and buildings.

7. B Area preference is sometimes referred to as location, location, location.

8. A The coop and tool shed would be considered trade fixtures and the tenant has the right to remove them up to the end of the lease.

9. C Man-made permanent attachments are called improvements.

10. C Appurtenances are rights and improvements attached to and traveling with the property ownership.

11. B Whether or not an item is real or personal property may be determined by intent, method of annexation, adaptation or agreement of the parties.

12. D Land cannot be destroyed although the improvements might be removed, as they are in this case.

13. D Real estate licensees should be careful not to "practice" law unless they are, in fact, licensed attorneys.

14 B While H might say the other things, B is correct in assuming that lighting fixtures are normally part of the real estate. If H had wanted to remove the fixtures, he should have done so before he put the house on the market, or written his intention into the agreement of sale.

15. A A real estate owner has the inherent right to exclude others from the property, although this right is not absolute. An adjacent property owner may have an easement right to use the property.

Property Description	Type of Property		Fixture	Trade Fixture
	Real	Personal		
1. Sidewalks and sewers in a subdivision	√			
2. Bushes surrounding a residence	√			
3. Wheat or corn crops on a farm		√		
4. Kitchen sink installed in a home	√		√	
5. Booths in a restaurant installed by a tenant		√		√
6. Curtains installed by a tenant		√		
7. Pumps installed by a gas station tenant		√		√
8. Machinery installed by landowner	√		√	
9. Crystal chandelier hung from the ceiling	√		√	
10. 80 gallon water heater with fiberglas insulating jacket	√		√	

Concepts of Home Ownership

3

Matching

Write the matching term on the appropriate line.

- apartment complex
- actual cash value
- coinsurance
- planned unit development
- cooperative
- mixed-use development
- condominium
- equity
- $500,000
- standard homeowner's insurance

1. ______________ A group of low-rise or high-rise rental residences that may include a number of amenities
2. ______________ A multiunit residential building owned by a corporation or trust and operated on behalf of stockholder/tenants who hold proprietary leases
3. ______________ A package insurance policy against loss due to fire, theft and liability
4. ______________ Amount excluded from capital gains tax for profits on sale of principle residence by married taxpayers filing jointly
5. ______________ A multiunit residential building in which individual units are owned in fee simple, plus an undivided joint interest in the common elements
6. ______________ Merging of diverse land uses into a subdivision or development
7. ______________ Interest or value an owner has in property over and above any indebtedness on that property
8. ______________ Clause in an insurance policy that requires the property to be insured at 80 percent of its replacement cost
9. ______________ In insurance, replacement value minus depreciation
10. ______________ High-rise development that combines commercial and residential uses in a single structure

True or False

Circle the answer

1. T F Under the traditional rule of thumb used by lenders to determine whether a prospective buyer can afford a home, PITI should not exceed 28 percent of gross monthly income, and payment on all debts should not exceed 36 percent of gross monthly income.

2. T F Under the rule of thumb traditionally used by lenders to determine whether or not a prospective buyer can afford a home, expenses such as insurance premiums, utilities and routine medical care are considered to be covered by a buyer's excess monthly income.

3. T F A cooperative is a form of residential ownership in which residents share ownership of common areas while owning their own units individually.

4. T F Warehouses, factories, office buildings, hotels and other structures that have been converted to residential use are referred to as planned unit developments.

5. T F Single taxpayers are entitled to a $250,000 exclusion from capital gains tax for profits on the sale of a principle residence.

6. T F The $250,000 exclusion from capital gains tax for profits on the sale of a principle residence can only be used once in a lifetime.

7. T F First-time buyers can borrow up to $10,000 from their tax-deferred IRAs without penalty.

8. T F Under standard homeowner's insurance policies, the insured is usually required to maintain insurance equal to at least 41 percent of the replacement cost of the dwelling, including the price of the land.

9. T F If a borrower's property is located in a designated flood area, there are no exemptions from the flood insurance requirement under the National Flood Insurance Act.

10. T F Equity represents the "paid off" share of a property, held free of any mortgage.

Check the Ads

On the numbered lines below write the types of housing indicated by each ad.

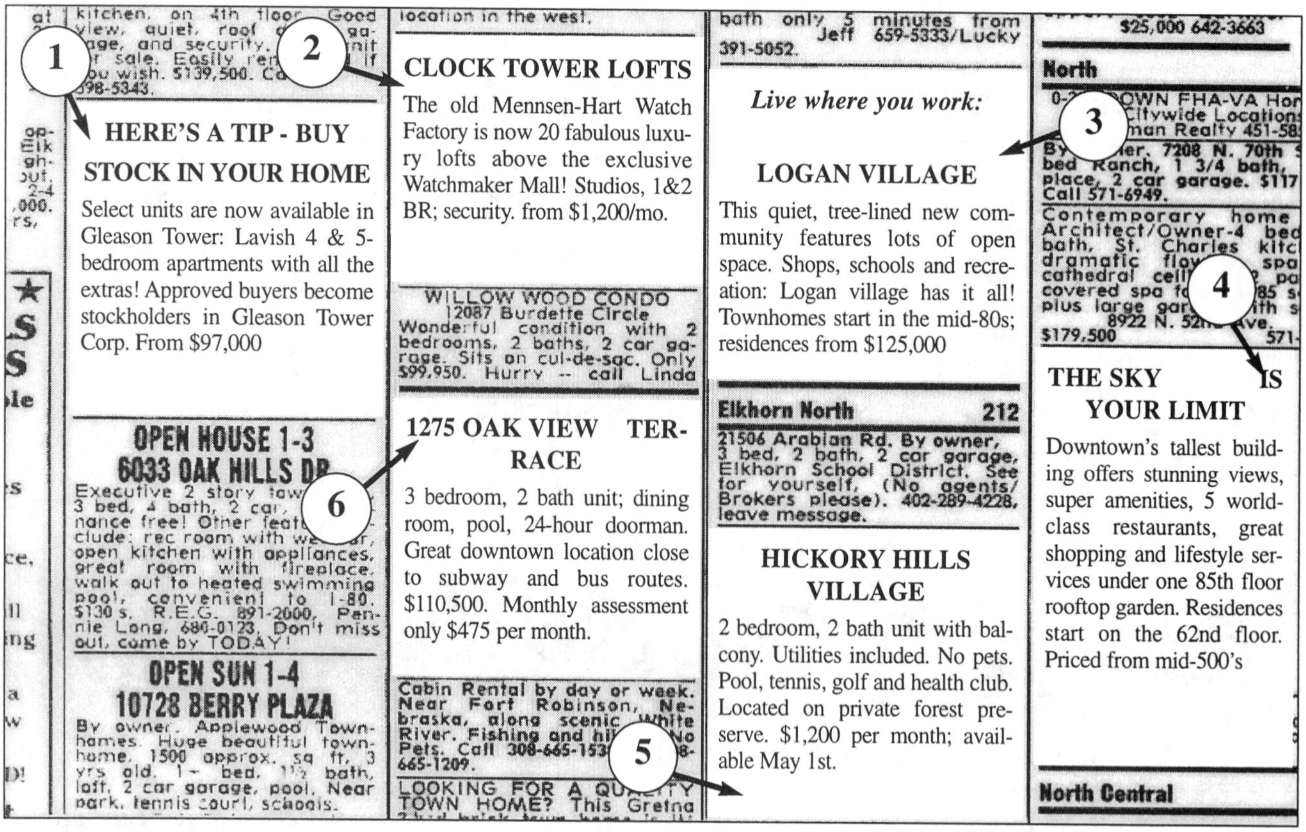

HERE'S A TIP - BUY STOCK IN YOUR HOME

Select units are now available in Gleason Tower: Lavish 4 & 5-bedroom apartments with all the extras! Approved buyers become stockholders in Gleason Tower Corp. From $97,000

CLOCK TOWER LOFTS

The old Mennsen-Hart Watch Factory is now 20 fabulous luxury lofts above the exclusive Watchmaker Mall! Studios, 1&2 BR; security. from $1,200/mo.

WILLOW WOOD CONDO 12087 Burdette Circle Wonderful condition with 2 bedrooms, 2 baths, 2 car garage. Sits on cul-de-sac. Only $99,950. Hurry -- call Linda

1275 OAK VIEW TERRACE

3 bedroom, 2 bath unit; dining room, pool, 24-hour doorman. Great downtown location close to subway and bus routes. $110,500. Monthly assessment only $475 per month.

Live where you work:

LOGAN VILLAGE

This quiet, tree-lined new community features lots of open space. Shops, schools and recreation: Logan village has it all! Townhomes start in the mid-80s; residences from $125,000

Elkhorn North 212

21506 Arabian Rd. By owner, 3 bed, 2 bath, 2 car garage, Elkhorn School District. See for yourself. (No agents/Brokers please). 402-289-4228, leave message.

HICKORY HILLS VILLAGE

2 bedroom, 2 bath unit with balcony. Utilities included. No pets. Pool, tennis, golf and health club. Located on private forest preserve. $1,200 per month; available May 1st.

THE SKY IS YOUR LIMIT

Downtown's tallest building offers stunning views, super amenities, 5 world-class restaurants, great shopping and lifestyle services under one 85th floor rooftop garden. Residences start on the 62nd floor. Priced from mid-500's

OPEN HOUSE 1-3 6033 OAK HILLS DR

OPEN SUN 1-4 10728 BERRY PLAZA

North

North Central

1. ____________ 3. ____________ 5. ____________

2. ____________ 4. ____________ 6. ____________

Flash Cards (Pull out page & cut with scissors)

capital gain	National Flood Insurance Act
coinsurance clause	Mixed Unit Developments (MUD)
condominiums	Planned Unit Developments (PUD)
cooperatives	replacement cost
equity	standard homeowners insurance
liability coverage	time shares

Requires flood insurance when financing with federally related loans on properties located in flood-prone areas

Chapter 3

Profit earned from the sale of an asset

Chapter 3

Often self contained, combine variety of uses from commercial to retail to residential

Chapter 3

Requires policyholder to maintain fire insurance coverage equal to at least 80% of property's actual replacement value

Chapter 3

Planned combination of diverse land uses, such as housing, recreation and shopping, in one contained development or subdivision

Chapter 3

Ownership of the airspace of a unit, plus undivided interest in common elements

Chapter 3

Current cost to reconstruct a building to serve the same function but not an exact duplicate of the original

Chapter 3

Multitenant building owned by trust or corporation; tenants own share of stock and proprietary lease

Chapter 3

Insurance package that covers residential property owner against financial loss from fire, theft, public liability, etc.

Chapter 3

The interest an owner has in a property over and above any outstanding loans.
(Market Value - Loans = Equity)

Chapter 3

Buy or lease the use of the property for a certain time frame - often used in resort areas

Chapter 3

Insurance protecting property owner in case of damage to a person or another's property due to owner's negligence

Chapter 3

Multiple Choice

Circle A, B, C or D

1. What is equity?
   A. Profit realized from the sale or exchange of real property
   B. Total amount of principal and interest plus tax and insurance
   C. Difference between the amount owed on a mortgage and the property's market value
   D. Amount of gain that may be deferred for income tax purposes

2. Which type of residence, depending on state law, may be considered either real or personal property?
   A. Converted-use properties
   B. Condominiums
   C. High-rise residential units
   D. Mobile homes

3. K's homeowner's insurance policy contains a coinsurance provision; the house is insured for replacement cost. If K's home burns down, which of the following statements is true?
   A. K's claim will be settled for the actual cash value of the damage.
   B. K's claim will be prorated by dividing the percentage of replacement cost by the minimum coverage requirement.
   C. K may make a claim for the full cost of the repair without deduction for depreciation.
   D. K may make a claim for the depreciated value of the damage.

4. Mr. and Mrs. Jones purchased their home in 1995 for $135,000. Now, they are being transferred to a new city and must sell their home, currently valued at $235,000. They are 52 and 53 respectively and are concerned about paying capital gains on their apparent profit of $100,000. Which of the following statements is important to them?
   A. No taxes are due since they have lived there more than two years and the gain is under the allowed amount.
   B. There is no problem as long as they purchase a new home for $235,000 or more within the next 24 months.
   C. They will have to pay taxes on their gain because neither is 55 or older in order to take advantage of the one-time exclusion of $125,000.
   D. They will have to pay taxes if the new home costs less than $235,000.

5. A high-rise building that includes office space, stores and residential units is an example of a
   A. loft building.
   B. master plan community.
   A. planned unit development.
   D. mixed-use development.

6. R, a single person, was born on July 10, 1944, and has lived in the same house for the past 5 years. When R sells the house on July 12, 1999, any gain from the sale of the home
   A. will be taxed at a lower rate because of R's age.
   B. will not be deferred, because R has lived in the house for fewer than 8 years.
   C. is excluded from taxation if it is less than $250,000.
   D. is excluded from income taxation up to $125,000 because of R's age and time-in-residence.

7. A real estate license may be required to broker a sale of a mobile home if it is classified as
   A. real property.
   B. personal property.
   C. converted use property.
   D. conditional use zoning.

8. T's house is constructed so that the floor of his home is built several inches above the 100-year flood mark. If T applies for a federally related mortgage loan, T's mortgage lender
   A. may exempt T's house from the flood insurance requirement.
   B. must require flood insurance.
   C. is prohibited by federal law from requiring flood insurance.
   D. may invoke the National Flood Insurance Act for properties lying inside, or within 500 feet of, a designated flood-prone area.

9. B, a prospective buyer, wants to purchase a house. His gross monthly income is $6,500. Assuming no debts, and if the lender uses a strict rule-of-thumb method, what is the maximum monthly PITI payment that B can afford?
   A. $1,635
   B. $1,775
   C. $1,820
   D. $2,340

Multiple Choice (Continued)

10. All of the following expenses may be deducted from a homeowner's gross income for income tax purposes EXCEPT
    A. loan repayment penalties.
    B. loan discount points.
    C. interest paid on overdue real estate taxes.
    D. real estate taxes.

11. A couple is planning to purchase a house. She earns $45,000 and he earns $37,500 per year. Their college loan payments total $350 per month and a car payment is $375 per month. Using a strict rule-of-thumb method, what is the maximum amount of PITI that they qualify for?
    A. $1,750
    B. $1,925
    C. $2,475
    D. $2,818

12. The buyers just paid $265,000 for their new home. The lot is valued at $30,000 and the mortgage loan is $198,000. How much equity do they have in this home?
    A. $53,000
    B. $67,000
    C. $212,000
    D. $235,000

13. A standard homeowner's insurance policy generally covers all of the following EXCEPT
    A. frozen pipes.
    B. vandalism.
    C. flooding.
    D. theft.

14. The reason that homeowners buy homeowner's insurance is to
    A. be reimbursed for financial losses suffered because of fire or theft.
    B. pay for replacing the furnace or roof because of age.
    C. be reimbursed for monetary losses due to a defect in the title.
    D. protect the homeowner for accidents on other people's property.

15. All of the following have contributed to a decline among first time buyers and low-to-moderate income purchases EXCEPT
    A. rising real estate prices.
    B. penalty-free withdrawals from IRA for the down payment.
    C. difficulties in saving the down payment.
    D. high level of consumer debt.

Answer Key

KEY TERM MATCHING

1. apartment complex
2. cooperative
3. standard homeowner's insurance
4. $500,000
5. condominium
6. planned unit development
7. equity
8. coinsurance
9. actual cash value
10. mixed-use development

TRUE or FALSE

1. True
2. True
3. False A condominium is a form of residential ownership in which residents share ownership of common areas while owning their own units individually.
4. False Warehouses, factories, office buildings, hotels and other structures that have been remodeled to residential use are referred to as converted use properties.
5. True
6. False The exemption may be used repeatedly, so long as the homeowners occupy the property as their primary residence for at least two years.
7. True

Answer Key (Continued)

8. False — Under standard homeowner's insurance policies, the insured is usually required to maintain insurance equal to at least 80 percent of the replacement cost of the dwelling, excluding the price of the land.

9. False — If a borrower's property is located in a designated flood area, it may be exempt from the National Flood Insurance Act's flood insurance requirement if the borrower can produce a survey showing that the lowest part of the structure is above the 100-year flood mark.

10. True

CHECKING THE ADS

1. cooperative
2. converted use
3. planned unit development
4. mixed use development
5. apartment complex
6. condominium

MULTIPLE CHOICE

1. C — Equity is the difference between market value and the money owed.

2. D — On the lot, a mobile home is considered personal property, but when it is moved to and installed on a site, it may be considered real property depending on local or state law.

3. C — Since K has insured the property for replacement value and has a coinsurance clause, K may make a claim for the full cost of replacement without deduction for depreciation.

4. A — Mr. and Mrs. Jones have lived in the home more than two years and their capital gain is less than $500,000, so they will not have to pay any capital gains tax.

5. D — A planned unit development is also referred to as a master plan community. A loft building is a less-than-complete answer. A mixed use development is usually a high-rise offering a mixture of uses.

6. C — Under the Tax Reform Act of 1997, R will not have to pay any tax because he has lived there for more than two years and the gain is less than $250,000.

7. A — If the mobile home is classified as real property, the agent selling the home generally must have a real estate license.

8. A — Because the lowest level is several inches above the 100-year-flood mark, the owner may not be required to buy flood insurance.

9. C — $6,500 x 28% = $1,820

10. C — Interest paid on overdue taxes may not be deducted from taxable income.

11. A — $45,000 + $37,500 = $82,500 annual ÷ 12 = $6,875 monthly income. $6,875 x 28% = $1,925. $6,875 x 36% = $2,475 – $350 – $375 = $1,750. Because of the debts, they will qualify for a lower amount.

12. B — $265,000– $198,000 = $67,000 equity

13. C — Most homeowner's insurance policies cover many perils, but not flooding. Flood insurance generally must be purchased separately.

14. A — Homeowner's insurance is purchased to protect the property owner from financial losses caused by events such as fire, theft or vandalism. It does not pay for routine maintenance, title defects or accidents on other people's property.

15. B — Penalty-free withdrawals from IRAs for first-time buyers' down payments are expected to promote their entry into home ownership. The other answers are contributing to the decline in home ownership.

4 Agency

Matching (A)

Write the matching term on the appropriate line.

- nonagent
- customer
- fiduciary relationship
- special agent
- agent
- general agent
- implied agency
- law of agency
- puffing
- principal

1. ______________ The basic framework that governs the legal responsibilities of an agent to a principal
2. ______________ An agent who is authorized to represent the principal in one specific act or business transaction, under detailed instructions
3. ______________ The individual who is authorized and consents to represent the interests of another person
4. ______________ The establishment of an agency relationship as the result of the actions of the parties
5. ______________ The individual who hires and delegates to the agent the responsibility of representing his or her interests
6. ______________ A relationship of trust and confidence as between a principal and an agent
7. ______________ Nonfraudulent exaggeration of a property's benefits or features
8. ______________ An agent authorized to represent the principal in a broad range of matters related to a specific business or activity
9. ______________ In a real estate agency relationship, the third party who is entitled to honesty and fair dealing
10. ______________ An intermediary between a buyer and seller who assists both parties with a transaction, but who represents neither party

True or False

Circle the answer

1. T F The individual who hires and delegates to the agent the responsibility of representing his or her other interests is the fiduciary.
2. T F Facilitators, transaction brokers, transaction coordinators and contract brokers are all examples of nonagents.
3. T F An agent works with a client and for the customer.
4. T F Under the common law of agency, the agent owes his or her principal the five duties of care, obedience, accounting, loyalty and disclosure.
5. T F The common law fiduciary duty of obedience obligates the agent to act in good faith at all times and obey all the principal's instructions.

Flash Cards (Pull out page & cut with scissors)

agent	negligent misrepresentation
errors and omissions insurance	puffing
fiduciary relationship	principal
fraud	special agent
general agent	stigmatized property
latent defect	subagent

Misrepresentation occurring when the broker should have known that the statement about a material fact was false

Chapter 4

Person who is hired to act for another. Hired by the principal

Chapter 4

Exaggerated comments about a property: "This is the best view of the valley."

Chapter 4

Liability insurance to cover broker for errors and negligence in general business; usually does not cover civil rights or antitrust violations

Chapter 4

One who hires; in real estate, the broker (principal) hires salespeople; seller (principal) hires the broker/agent; or buyer (principal) hires broker/agent

Chapter 4

Relationship of trust and confidence between principal and agent; agent owes duties of care, obedience, accounting, loyalty and disclosure

Chapter 4

Agent hired by principal to perform a single act. In real estate, broker is special agent hired by seller to find ready, willing, able buyer

Chapter 4

Intentional misrepresentation of a material fact in order to harm or take advantage of another person

Chapter 4

Property branded as undesirable because of an event that happened there, such as murder, suicide, drug dealing

Chapter 4

Agent hired to represent principal in specific range of matters: long-term, broad authority

Chapter 4

Agent working for an agent; in real estate, the salesperson is the broker's agent and subagent to the seller (or buyer)

Note - Not permitted in some states

Chapter 4

Hidden structural defect that would not be discovered by ordinary inspection

Chapter 4

True or False (Continued)

6. T F The common law duty of loyalty requires that an agent not disclose the principal's financial situation or facts about the condition of the property.

7. T F The source of compensation is the key determining factor in whether or not an agency relationship exists.

8. T F Universal agents are empowered to do anything their principals can do personally, with virtually no limitation on their authority to act.

9. T F A real estate broker is usually the general agent of a buyer or seller.

10. T F The only difference between a buyer's agent and a seller's agent is that a buyer's agent owes the principal different fiduciary duties.

11. T F In a dual agency relationship, the agent represents two principals in the same transaction.

12. T F A dual agency relationship is legal if either the buyer or the seller consents to the dual representation.

13. T F An agent owes a customer the duties of reasonable care and skill, honest and fair dealing, and disclosure of known facts.

14. T F A negligent misrepresentation occurs when the broker engages in exaggeration of a property's benefits or features.

15. T F When a property has a hidden structural defect that could not be discovered by ordinary inspection, it is referred to as a stigmatized property.

Matching (B)

Write the matching term on the appropriate line.

- disclosed dual agency
- common law agent duties
- buyers' agents
- client
- undisclosed dual agency
- latent defect
- stigmatized property
- subagent
- express agreement
- universal agent

1. ________________ An agency relationship in which the agent represents two principals simultaneously, without their knowledge or permission
2. ________________ A contract in which the parties formally state their intention to establish an agency relationship
3. ________________ Real estate licensees who represent buyers exclusively
4. ________________ An agent empowered to do anything the principal could do personally
5. ________________ A property that has been branded as undesirable because of the events that occurred in or near it
6. ________________ The principal in a real estate agency relationship
7. ________________ An agency relationship in which the agent represents two principals simultaneously, with their knowledge or permission
8. ________________ Care, obedience, accounting, loyalty and disclosure
9. ________________ The party to whom an agent delegates some of his or her authority
10. ________________ A hidden structural problem that would not be discovered by ordinary inspection

Multiple Choice

Circle A, B, C or D

1. An individual who is authorized and consents to represent the interests of another person is a(n)
   A. client.
   B. principal.
   C. agent.
   D. facilitator.

2. Broker N represents C, but is currently working with K to find a home. Assuming that no statute has replaced the traditional common law, which of the following correctly identifies the parties in this relationship?
   A. N is K's agent; C is N's client.
   B. K is N's client; C is N's principal.
   C. C is N's customer; K is N's client.
   D. N is C's agent; K is N's customer.

3. The agent's obligation to use his or her skill and expertise on behalf of the principal arises under which of the common-law duties?
   A. Care
   B. Obedience
   C. Loyalty
   D. Disclosure

4. An agent representing the seller has a duty to disclose to his or her principal all of the following EXCEPT
   A. ridiculously low offers.
   B. the buyer's financial ability to offer a higher price.
   C. the agent's advertising budget.
   D. the buyer's intention to resell the property for a profit.

5. J, a broker, has an agency agreement to represent the seller, M, in the sale of Grandview Mansion. The agreement's expiration date is June 10. On May 5, Grandview Mansion is struck by lightning and burns to the ground. M, overwhelmed by grief, dies. Based on these facts, which of the following is true?
   A. The agency agreement was terminated by the fire, although M's death also would have done so.
   B. The agency agreement was not terminated until M's death on June 11.
   C. If Grandview Mansion had not been destroyed by the fire, M's death would not have terminated the agreement; J would become the broker for M's estate.
   D. Only the mutual agreement of the parties can terminate a valid agency agreement before its expiration date.

6. A person who is designated by the principal in a broad range of matters related to a particular transaction or activity is a(n)
   A. universal agent.
   B. special agent.
   C. designated agent.
   D. general agent.

7. Z, a real estate broker, signed an agency agreement with a seller, V. The asking price for V's house was $98,500. A few days later, Z met Q at a charity dinner. Q was interested in buying a home in the $95,000 to $110,000 price range. Z agreed to help Q locate such a property and to represent Q in negotiating a favorable purchase price. Based on these facts, which of the following statements is true?
   A. Z's relationships with Q and V are separate issues, and no dual agency question arises.
   B. V is Z's client, and Q is Z's customer; there is no dual agency problem.
   C. Z has created a potential undisclosed dual agency problem, and should disclose the relationships to both parties before showing V's home to Q.
   D. Z has created a dual agency problem, and should immediately terminate the agreement with either V or Q.

8. Broker T is showing a house to a prospective buyer. T points out the "rustic charm" of the sagging front porch and refers to a weed-choked backyard as a "delightful garden." T is engaging in which of the following?
   A. Intentional misrepresentation
   B. Negligent misrepresentations
   C. Puffing
   D. Fraud

9. A house built over a ditch covered with decaying timber, or ceilings that are improperly attached to the support beams are examples of
   A. stigmatized properties.
   B. environmental hazards.
   C. latent defects.
   D. conditions that need not be disclosed.

10. The seller's agent has certain duties to the client/principal. All of the following are duties of the principal EXCEPT
    A. cooperation.
    B. compensation.
    C. marketing.
    D. disclosure.

Multiple Choice (Continued)

11. The seller asked the agent to "not show my house to any foreigners." In this circumstance, the agent
    A. must show the house to any one who wants to see it.
    B. must decline to take the listing with this requirement.
    C. may take the listing and ignore the instruction.
    D. may take the listing and hope that no foreigners ask to see the property.

12. Who is the agent's principal?
    A. Seller
    B. Buyer
    C. Person who pays the commission
    D. Whoever hired the agent

13. The broker was hired to represent the seller, to market the property, and to solicit offers to purchase. The broker is called a
    A. general agent.
    C. universal agent.
    B. special agent.
    D. nonagent.

14. The house was the scene of a drug bust and a violent murder. When it was put on the market, it was referred to as a
    A. latent property.
    B. stigmatized property.
    C. damaged property.
    D. property with a material defect.

15. All of the following will terminate an agency relationship EXCEPT
    A. death of either party.
    B. destruction of the property.
    C offer made on the property.
    D. expiration of the agreement.

Answer Key

MATCHING (A)

1. law of agency
2. special agent
3. agent
4. implied agency
5. principal
6. fiduciary relationship
7. puffing
8. general agent
9. customer
10. nonagent

TRUE OR FALSE

1. False — The individual who hires and delegates to the agent the responsibility of representing his other interests is the principal.
2. True
3. False — An agent works for the client and with the customer.
4. True
5. False — The common law fiduciary duty of obedience obligates the agent to act in good faith at all times and obey all the principal's lawful and ethical instructions.
6. False — The common law duty of loyalty requires that an agent not disclose the principal's financial situation but facts about the condition of the property must be disclosed.
7. False — The source of compensation is not the key determining factor in whether or not an agency relationship exists.
8. True
9. False — A real estate broker is usually the special agent of a buyer or seller.

Answer Key (Continued)

10. False — A buyer's agent owes his or her principal the same fiduciary duties as a seller's agent owes a seller.

11. True

12. False — A dual agency relationship is legal if both the buyer and the seller consent to the dual representation.

13. True

14. False — Puffing occurs when the broker engages in exaggeration of a property's benefits or features, OR A negligent misrepresentation occurs when the broker should have known that a statement about a material fact was false.

15. False — When a property has a hidden structural defect that could not be discovered by ordinary inspection, it is referred to as having a latent defect.

MATCHING ANSWERS (B)

1. undisclosed dual agency
2. express agreement
3. buyers' agents
4. universal agent
5. stigmatized property
6. client
7. disclosed dual agency
8. common law agent duties
9. subagent
10. latent defect

MULTIPLE CHOICE ANSWERS

1. C — The agent is hired by the principal who is also the agent's client.

2. D — Watch the terminology: the broker is working for (representing) C and is working with K (a customer) to find a home.

3. A — Care requires skill and expertise; obedience of lawful instructions, loyalty is putting the client's interests above the agents, and disclosure refers to material defects of the property.

4. C — The seller's [special] agent must present all offers, any facts about the buyer that would assist the seller in making a decision, including the fact that the buyer intends to resell the property.

5. A — Both destruction of the property and death of either party are reasons for termination of the agency agreement.

6. D — A special agent is given limited authority for a limited time. A general agent is given broad authority in a specific circumstance. A universal agent is given broad authority over a number of circumstances.

7. C — Z is representing the seller and now is at least implying that Z will represent the buyer in locating a property: hence two clients. If Z intends to show V's property, Z must disclose Z's relationship with both clients, gain their agreement to a dual agency, and only then proceed.

8. C — Since any prudent buyer can see the sagging porch and weed-choked garden, these are "puffing" statements. Agents must take care that they do not statements in such a way as to harm the buyer or take advantage of the buyer's ignorance, which would constitute fraud.

9. C — Problems with the property which cannot be observed by the normal person are called latent defects.

10. C — Marketing is the agent's responsibility. The principal who hired the agent is responsible for cooperating with the agent, disclosing material defects, and compensating the agent.

11. B — Under the common law agency responsibility of obedience, the agent must obey all lawful instructions. However, this is an instruction to violate the Fair Housing Laws. The agent should not take the listing and ignore the instruction, nor pretend that it doesn't exist.

Answer Key (Continued)

12. D The most complete answer is "whoever hired the agent." That could be either the buyer or the seller, but who pays the compensation is not the determining factor

13. B A special agent is one who is hired for a limited time and given limited authority. A broker taking a listing is generally a special agent.

14. B Presuming that the property is physically intact, the drug bust and violent murder may create psychological reactions to the property rendering it "stigmatized."

15. C An offer on the property does not terminate the agency relationship, but the death of either party, destruction of the property, or expiration of the term will.

5

Real Estate Brokerage

Matching

Write the matching term on the appropriate line.

- allocation of markets
- antitrust laws
- caveat emptor
- commission
- salesperson
- brokerage
- independent contractor
- rules and regulations
- employee
- ready, willing & able buyer
- real estate broker
- procuring cause
- group boycotting
- real estate license laws
- sole proprietorship

1. ______________ The common law doctrine of "let the buyer beware"
2. ______________ Statutes enacted by state legislatures to protect the public and ensure a standard of competence in the real estate industry
3. ______________ The device by which a state licensing authority defines and enforces the statutory law
4. ______________ The business of bringing parties together
5. ______________ An individual who is licensed to buy, sell, exchange or lease property for others, and to charge a fee for those services
6. ______________ Company held by a single owner
7. ______________ A person who is licensed only to perform real estate activities on behalf of a broker
8. ______________ A salesperson whose activities are closely controlled, and who is entitled to benefits, unemployment compensation and income tax withholding
9. ______________ A licensee who works under the terms of a written contract and receives more than 90 percent of his or her income from sales production rather than hours worked
10. ______________ A form of compensation computed as a percentage of the total sales price of a property
11. ______________ The broker who starts an uninterrupted chain of events that results in the sale of a property
12. ______________ A person who is prepared to buy on the seller's terms
13. ______________ A conspiracy by two or more businesses against another
14. ______________ An illegal division of territories to avoid competition
15. ______________ Law that prohibits price fixing and tie-in agreements

Flash Cards (Pull out page & cut with scissors)

antitrust laws	price fixing
commission	procuring cause
employee	rules and regulations
group boycotts	sole proprietorship
independent contractor	transaction broker
license laws	tying arrangements

Brokers conspiring to set fixed compensation rates

Chapter 5

Laws to minimize unfair competition. Illegal to conspire to fix prices, allocate customers or markets.

Chapter 5

In order to be paid, the broker starts an uninterrupted chain of events that results in a sale

Chapter 5

Payment to broker for services rendered. In the sale of real property, often a percentage of the selling price

Chapter 5

Licensing authority to provide for administering the law and set operating guidelines for licensees. Have the same force and effect as any law

Chapter 5

Works for employer who is responsible for withholding income taxes and FICA

Chapter 5

Single owner company

Chapter 5

Illegal antitrust activity. Two or more businesses conspire against another business or agree not to work with another company in order to reduce competition

Chapter 5

Intermediary between buyer and seller who assists both parties, though not an agent of either. AKA nonagent, facilitator, coordinator or contract broker

Chapter 5

Person hired to perform a certain act, only end result is under control and direction of another. Most real estate licensees are treated as independent contractors.

Chapter 5

Illegal antitrust activity. Agreement to sell one product only if the buyer purchases another product as well

Chapter 5

State laws enacted to protect the public by ensuring a standard of competence and professionalism in the real estate industry

Chapter 5

Circle the answer — True or False

1. T F Only a few states regulate the activities of real estate brokers and salespeople.

2. T F The purpose of the real estate license laws is to regulate the real estate industry and protect the constitutional rights of property owners.

3. T F A real estate salesperson is licensed to buy, sell, exchange or lease real property for others, and to charge a fee for those services.

4. T F The Internal Revenue Service has established criteria for determining whether a real estate licensee is classified as an employee or an independent contractor for income tax purposes.

5. T F The amount of a broker's compensation is always negotiable.

6 T F A real estate salesperson is an individual who is licensed to perform real estate activities on behalf of a licensed broker.

7. T F A broker is considered to be the procuring cause of a sale if he or she is present at the time the transaction closes.

8. T F Price-fixing, group boycotting and allocation of markets are three examples of antitrust violations.

9. T F The practice of setting standard prices for products or services is referred to as a tie-in arrangement.

10. T F In a civil suit based on an antitrust violation by a real estate licensee, the injured party may recover three times the value of actual damages.

Who's Who?

Based on their statements below, place each speaker's name in the appropriate box of Open Door Realty's organizational chart

Figure 5.1

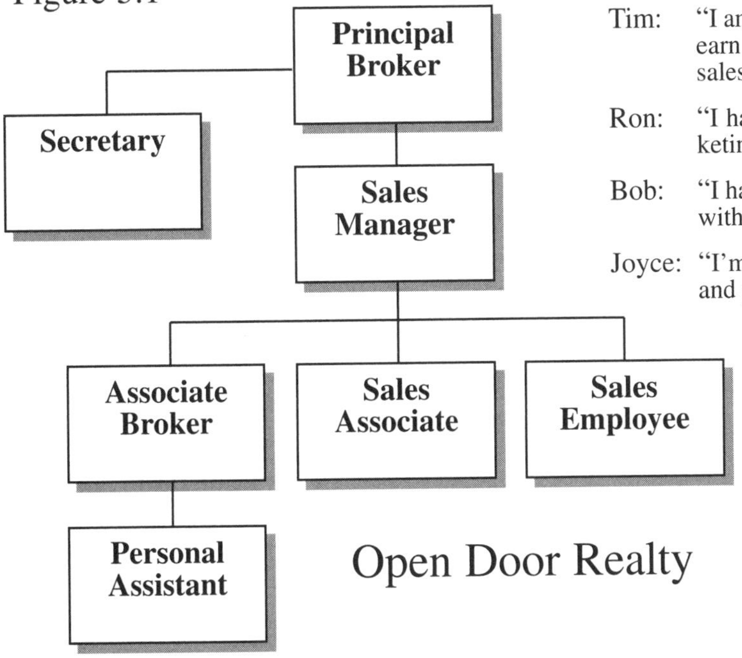

Tim: "I am a licensed real estate salesperson. I work for Bob and earn half my income from an hourly salary and half from sales."

Ron: "I have a real estate license, but my job is limited to marketing and office management activities."

Bob: "I have a real estate broker's license. I work under contract with the broker and earn all of my income from sales."

Joyce: "I'm a licensed real estate salesperson. I set my own hours and pay my own taxes."

Elaine: "I am a broker licensed to buy, sell, exchange ore lease real property for a fee. I am responsible for the trust account."

Sandra: "I am licensed to perform real estate activities on behalf of a broker. I have health insurance and a retirement plan."

Dora: "Although I don't have a real estate license, I work closely with the licensees to ensure that the office runs smoothly and transactions go to closing."

Multiple Choice

Circle A, B, C or D

1. Real estate license laws have been enacted in all 50 states. The purpose of these laws is to
   A. protect licensees from lawsuits.
   B. protect the public and establish standards of professionalism.
   C. protect the public and prevent licensees from engaging in profit-making activities.
   D. establish maximum levels of competency and a moral marketplace.

2. In real estate, a salesperson is a(n)
   A. independent contractor.
   B. employee of a licensed broker.
   C. licensee who performs real estate activities on behalf of a broker.
   D. combination office manager, marketer and organizer with a fundamental understanding of the real estate industry, who may or may not be licensed.

3. All of the following are the indicators of independent contractor status used by the Internal Revenue Service, EXCEPT
   A. a current real estate license.
   B. specific hours stated in a written agreement.
   C. a written agreement that specifies that the individual will not be treated as an employee for tax purposes.
   D. 90 percent or more of the individual's income is based on sales production rather than hours worked.

4. The broker who owns Happy Homes Realty does not permit his salespeople to charge less than an 8 percent commission in any transaction. After reading a newspaper article about Happy Homes' policies, the broker of Open Door Homefinders decides to adopt the 8 percent minimum, too. Based on these facts, which of the following statements is true?
   A. Happy Homes policy is price fixing and violates the antitrust law.
   B. Although Happy Homes original policy was legal, Open Door's adoption of the minimum commission may constitute an antitrust violation if both brokers are in the same real estate market.
   C. Both brokers engaged in illegal price fixing.
   D. Neither broker has committed an antitrust violation.

5. A real estate broker had a listing agreement with a seller that specified a 6 percent commission. The broker showed the home to a prospective buyer. The next day, the buyer called the seller directly and offered to buy the house for 5 percent less than the asking price. The seller agreed to the price, and informed the broker in writing that no further brokerage services would be required. The sale went to closing six weeks later. Based on these facts, which of the following statements is true?
   A. While the broker was the procuring cause of the sale, the seller properly canceled the contract; without a valid employment agreement in force at the time of closing, the broker is not entitled to a commission.
   B. The broker is entitled to a partial commission, and the buyer is obligated to pay it.
   C. Under the facts as stated, the broker is not the procuring cause of this sale but is still entitled to a commission.
   D. The broker was the procuring cause of this sale, and is entitled to the full 6 percent commission.

6. A qualified buyer makes a written offer on a property on March 6 by filling out and signing a sales agreement. Later that day, the seller accepts and signs the agreement, keeping one copy. The broker gives a copy of the signed agreement to the buyer on March 8. The seller's deed is delivered on May 1. The deed is recorded on May 7, and the buyer takes possession on May 15. When is the broker's commission payable if this is a "usual" transaction?
   A. March 8
   B. May 1
   C. May 7
   D. May 15

7. All of the following are violations of the federal antitrust laws EXCEPT
   A. group boycotting.
   B. allocation of customers.
   C. commission splitting.
   D. tying agreements.

8. All of the following are ways for the broker to charge for services EXCEPT
   A. agreed upon rate with other brokers.
   B. flat fees.
   C. hourly rate.

***Multiple Choice** (Continued)*

9. What is the main value of a multiple listing service (MLS)?
   A. Agents do not have to work so hard to locate properties.
   B. Slows down selling activities
   C. Very little cooperation among brokers
   D. Exposes the property to a greater number of prospective buyers

10. License laws are enacted by the legislature. Who is responsible for rule and regulations?
   A. Small committee that reports to the legislature
   B. Local REALTOR®, association
   C. Licensing authority (division, commission, etc.)
   D. Brokers and salespeople appointed by the governor

Math Practice

Circle A, B, C or D

1. J listed and sold her property for $238,000. She agreed to pay the listing broker a 7 percent commission. The listing broker offered a listing 40/60 selling split to any cooperating broker who sold the property. How much did J have to pay in commission fees?
   A. $6,664
   B. $9,996
   C. $16,660
   D. Not enough information

2. The salesperson's agreement with the broker was a 40/60 split with the broker keeping 40 percent of the commission. The seller was charged 5.5 percent. How much did the salesperson receive if she listed and sold a house for $179,500?
   A. $3,949
   B. $8,975
   C. $9,872.50
   D. None of the above

3. The broker listed B's home for $325,000 with a 4 percent commission plus $2,000 for advertising costs. The buyer offered $280,000 and after several counteroffers, finally agreed to $300,000. What was the total cost to the seller?
   A. $11,200
   B. $13,000
   C. $14,000
   D. $18,000

4. Salespeople in PQR Realty are compensated based on the following formula: 35 percent of the com-mission earned on any sale, less a $150 per transaction desk rental. Salespeople are responsible for paying 75 percent of all marketing and sales expenses for any property they list, and a $50 per transaction fee to cover the monthly expenses of advertising and marketing PQR's services.

   If a salesperson sold a house for $128,000, with a 6 percent commission, how much would he or she be paid if the sale incurred $347.75 in marketing and advertising costs?
   A. $2,227.19
   B. $2,246.09
   C. $2,545.62
   D. $7,273.19

5. At Sure Sale Realty, salespeople pay a monthly desk rent of 15 percent of their monthly income. In May, one salesperson receives 6 percent on a $95,000 sale, 7.5 percent on a $105,250 sale and 6.75 percent on an $89,500 sale. The only other salesperson at Sure Sale who received a commission in May got 7 percent on a $128,000 sale. How much did Sure Sale Realty receive in May?
   A. $4,289.25
   B. $7,095.97
   C. $12,251.53
   D. $14,945.00

State License Requirements

Figure 5.2

Fill in the license requirements in the table below based on your state's license laws, rules and regulations.

REQUIREMENTS	SALES LICENSE	BROKER LICENSE
Age		
Education		
Experience		
Bond		
Credit Report		
Recommendations		
Photograph		
Fingerprints		
Continuing Education		
Licensure Period		
Expiration Date		

Answer Key

MATCHING ANSWERS

1. caveat emptor
2. real estate license laws
3. rules and regulations
4. brokerage
5. real estate broker
6. sole proprietorship
7. salesperson
8. employee
9. independent contractor
10. commission
11. procuring cause
12. ready, willing, and able buyer
13. group boycott
14. allocation of markets
15. antitrust laws

TRUE OR FALSE

1. False — All 50 states somehow regulate the activities of real estate brokers and salespeople.
2. False — The purpose of the real estate license laws is to regulate the real estate industry and protect the rights of purchasers, sellers, tenants and owners.
3. False — A real estate broker is licensed to buy, sell, exchange or lease real property for others, and to charge a fee for those services.
4. True
5. True
6. True

Answer Key (Continued)

7. False A broker is considered the procuring cause of a sale if he or she started an uninterrupted chain of events that resulted in the sale.
8. True
9. False Price fixing is the practice of competitors setting prices for products or services.
10. True

WHO'S WHO *(Figure 5.1)*

1. Principal Broker	Elaine
2. Secretary	Dora
3. Sales Manager	Ron
4. Associate Broker	Bob
5. Sales Associate	Joyce
6. Sales Employee	Sandra
7. Personal Assistant	Tim

MULTIPLE CHOICE

1. B Licensees will face lawsuits if they ignore the laws. C is partially correct (protect the public) but licensees may engage in profit-making activities. D is incorrect; minimum levels of competency are established.
2. C While the salesperson is treated as an independent contractor for income tax purposes, the salesperson must still work directly under the broker's name. D is the definition of a personal assistant.
3. B A, C, and D are IRS requirements. Number of hours may not be specified.
4. D Since the Open Door broker learned about Happy Homes' policies from a public source, that is, the newspaper, and without discussing the policy with Happy Homes, neither broker has committed an antitrust violation.
5. D Obviously, the broker introduced a ready, willing and able buyer to the seller prior to the seller's cancelation of the listing agreement and thus is entitled to the commission.
6. B Although the commission was earned when the buyer was notified of the seller's acceptance (March 8), the commission is typically paid at the time the deed is delivered.
7. C It is legal for agents to share and split commissions. Price fixing, allocation of customers and group boycotting are illegal under the antitrust laws.
8. A Under antitrust laws, brokers may not get together and agree to charge the same rates to consumers. Brokers may charge for services using a flat fee, an hourly rate, or a commission based on a percentage of the selling price.
9. D The MLS exposes the property to many different agents, encouraging cooperation among brokers and expediting sales.
10. C Rules and regulations are written and adopted by the licensing authorities in each state. They have the same force as the law, but are easier to change since they do not have to go through the legislature.

MATH PRACTICE ANSWERS:

1. C What the brokers agree to regarding splitting the commission is not relevant to the total cost to the seller. $238,000 x 7% = $16,600
2. D $179,500 X 5.5% x 60% = $5,923.50 (Some exams will do this to you.)
3. C $300,000 x 4% + $2,000 = $14,000
4. A $128,000 X 6% = $7,680 x 35% = $2,688 less $150 less $50 less $260.81 ($347.75 x 75%) = $2,227.19
5. A $95,000 x 6% = $5,700
   $105,250 x 7.5% = $7,893.75
   $89,500 x 6.75% = $6,041.25
   $128,000 x 7% = $8,960
   $5,700 + $7,893.75 + $6,041.25 + $8,960 = $28,595 x 15% = $4,289.25

LICENSE REQUIREMENTS *(Figure 5.2)*

Each state will have different answers. Students should work together.

6 Listing Agreements and Buyer Representation

Matching

Write the matching term on the appropriate line.

- CMA
- option listing
- exclusive-agency listing
- exclusive buyer agency
- exclusive-right-to-sell listing
- listing agreement
- MLS
- net listing
- open buyer agency
- open listing

1. ______________ An employment contract for a broker's services
2. ______________ A listing agreement under which the seller must pay the broker a commission regardless of who sells the property
3. ______________ A listing agreement with a single broker, under which the seller retains the right to sell the property independently without being obligated to pay a commission
4. ______________ A listing agreement in which the seller may employ multiple brokers, retains the right to market the property independently, and is obligated to compensate only the broker who produces a buyer, if any
5. ______________ A marketing organization whose broker members make their own exclusive listings available to other brokers
6. ______________ A listing agreement in which the seller receives a specific dollar amount from the sales price, and the selling broker retains the balance as his or her compensation
7. ______________ A comparison of the sales prices of similar properties
8. ______________ A contract between a buyer and a buyer's broker that permits the buyer to enter into an unlimited number of similar agreements
9. ______________ A contract between a buyer and a buyer's broker in which the agent is entitled to compensation even if the buyer finds a suitable property independently
10. ______________ A listing agreement in which the broker has the right to purchase the listed property

True or False

Circle the answer

1. T F Under a typical net listing, the broker's commission is based on a percentage of the seller's net from the transaction.

2. T F A listing agreement is a contract for the sale of real estate.

Flash Cards (Pull out page & cut with scissors)

broker protection clause	indemnification
buyer agency agreement	market value
competitive market analysis (CMA)	multiple-listing service (MLS)
exclusive-agency listing agreement	net listing
exclusive-right-to-sell listing agreement	open listing
expiration of listing	option listing

In a listing, a clause that states that the seller and broker will not sue each other for any incorrect information supplied by one to the other

Chapter 6

Protects broker from buyer and seller making contract behind broker's back. Provides for commission if broker's buyer purchases within a period after listing expires

Chapter 6

Most probable price the property will sell for in an arm's-length transaction under normal conditions on the open market

Chapter 6

Employment contract in which the buyer hires the broker to find a property to buy. Broker owes fiduciary responsibilities to buyer/client

Chapter 6

Marketing organization in which brokers share information and commission with other brokers; sellers gain because of greater exposure to larger market

Chapter 6

Analysis of market activity among comparable properties; not an appraisal

Chapter 6

Broker entitled to any amount above the seller's stated net; often illegal; potential conflict of interest between broker's interest and seller's interest

Chapter 6

One agent (broker) is hired; broker receives a commission only if he or she is the procuring cause; seller retains right to sell without obligation to pay commission

Chapter 6

Multiple agents; only the selling agent (broker) entitled to commission; seller retains right to sell independently without obligation to pay anyone a commission

Chapter 6

One agent (broker) is hired; broker receives a commission regardless of who finds the buyer for the property

Chapter 6

Broker has the right to purchase the property; broker must be very honest to avoid charges of fraud

Chapter 6

Specific termination of listing; in most states, failure to specify specific date is grounds for suspension or revocation of license

Chapter 6

True or False (Continued)

3. T F The parties to a listing agreement are a broker or salesperson and a buyer or a seller.

4. T F The salesperson sets the listing price for a property by using a competitive market analysis.

5. T F A listing agreement in which the seller retains the right to employ any number of brokers as agent is referred to as a multiple listing.

6. T F In an exclusive-agency listing, one broker is authorized to act as the exclusive agent of the principal, who retains the right to sell the property without obligation to the broker.

7. T F In buyer agency, the source of compensation is the major factor that determines the relationship.

8. T F In an exclusive-right-to-sell listing, the seller must pay the broker's commission even if the seller finds a buyer without the broker's assistance.

9. T F In an exclusive buyer agency agreement, the broker is entitled to payment only if he or she locates the property that the buyer ultimately purchases.

10. T F Because a listing agreement is a personal service contract between a broker and seller, the broker may transfer the listing to another broker with or without the seller's consent.

Listing Contracts

Label each of the three diagrams below to indicate the type of listing contract it represents

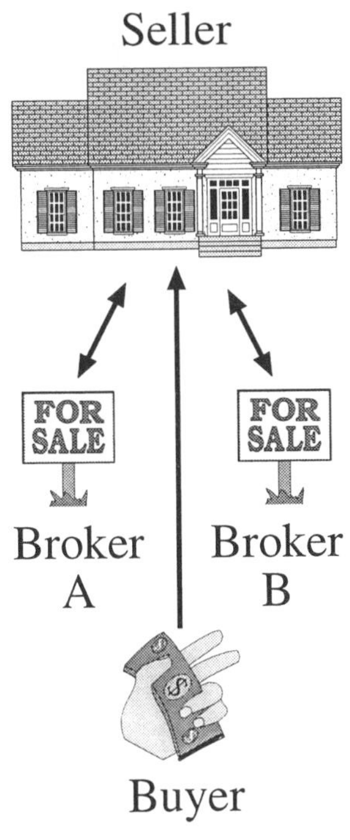

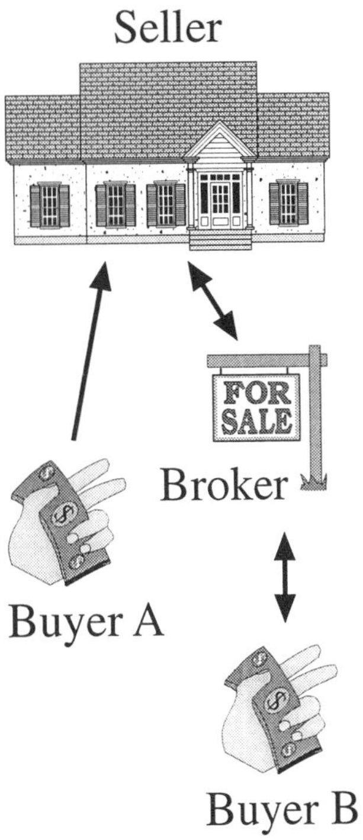

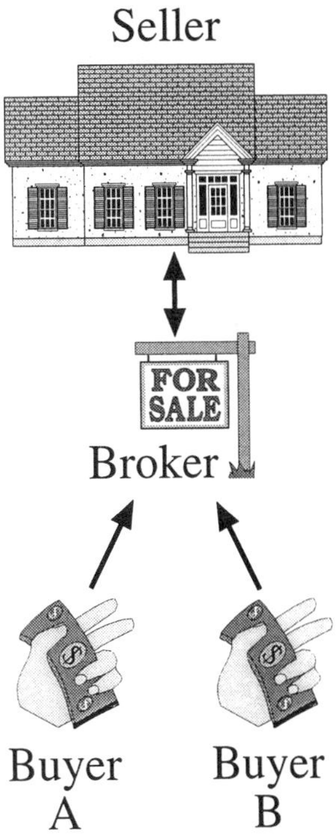

1. ______________ 2. ______________ 3. ______________

Multiple Choice

Circle A, B, C or D

1. In a typical buyer agency agreement, the buyer is the
   A. principal.
   B. customer.
   C. agent.
   D. employee.

2. The owner listed her home for sale with a broker. When the owner sold the home herself, she didn't owe anyone a commission. Based on these facts, what type of listing did the broker and the owner most likely sign?
   A. Exclusive-right-to-sell listing
   B. Net listing
   C. Multiple listing
   D. Open listing

3. All of the following information is generally included in a listing agreement EXCEPT
   A. lot dimensions.
   B. most recent year's property taxes.
   C. client's specific requirements for a suitable property.
   D. agency and property condition disclosures.

4. On January 10, a salesperson met with a seller and described the advantages of listing the seller's property with his broker's office. On January 15, the seller agreed to the listing: the salesperson and the seller signed the agreement. On January 18, the broker signed the listing agreement as required by office policy. On January 20, the salesperson posted a "For Sale" sign in front of the house. When did the listing agreement become effective?
   A. January 10
   B. January 15
   C. January 18
   D. January 20

5. The listed price of a property is always
   A. negotiable.
   B. a function of market value.
   C. the seller's decision.
   D. determined by a CMA.

6. What is a listing agreement?
   A. Contract between buyer and seller
   B. Contract to purchase real property
   C. Employment agreement between broker and salesperson
   D. Employment contract between seller and broker

7. Who are the parties to a listing agreement?
   A. Buyer and seller
   B. Seller and broker
   C. Seller and salesperson
   D. Buyer and salesperson

8. There are five different brokerage signs in the front yard. Evidently, the seller has signed a(n)
   A. exclusive-agency listing.
   B. exclusive-right-to-sell listing.
   C. net listing.
   D. open listing.

9. The broker has just explained the value of signing a listing with a broker who is a member of the multiple listing service. The broker is trying to overcome the objections of the seller who wants a(n)
   A. open listing.
   B. exclusive-agency listing.
   C. exclusive-right-to-sell listing.
   D. net listing.

10. What kind of listing agreement is illegal in most states because of the potential for conflict of interest between a broker's fiduciary responsibility to the seller and the broker's profit motive?
    A. Open listing
    B. Net listing
    C. Exclusive-right-to-sell listing
    D. Exclusive-agency listing

11. The buyer hired a broker to help locate a suitable property. However, on the way home from work, the buyer went by an open house, fell in love with it, and promptly signed purchase aagreement. The buyer was still obligated to pay the broker a commission because the original agreement was a(n)
    A. exclusive buyer agency agreement.
    B. exclusive-agency buyer agency agreement.
    C. net agency agreement.
    D. open buyer agency agreement.

12. Buyer agents will usually be compensated in all of the following ways EXCEPT
    A. flat fee for service.
    B. percentage of selling price.
    C. hourly rate.
    D. percentage of list price.

Multiple Choice (Continued)

13. The buyer's agent must obtain information from the buyer. All of the following would be useful to the buyer's agent EXCEPT
    A. detailed financial information.
    B. specific requirements for suitable property.
    C. how soon the buyer has to move.
    D. the cost of the buyer's previous home.

14. All of the following will terminate a listing agreement EXCEPT
    A. performance.
    B. expiration.
    C. an offer to purchase.
    D. abandonment by the broker.

15. A broker is retiring and wants to sell his listings to another broker. How can he do this?
    A. By signing over the listings to the new broker
    B. The new broker has to sign an acceptance agreement
    C. Each salesperson must sign over his or her listing to the new broker
    D. The sellers must agree to a new listing with the new broker

Math Practice

Circle A, B, C or D

1. The brokerage charged the seller $1,000 as an advertising fee and 4 percent of the selling price. The house was listed for $139,500 and sold for $129,350. What was the total amount the seller paid the brokerage?
    A. $5,174 C. $6,580
    B. $5,580 D. none of the above

2. The seller agreed to a 5 percent commission on a sale price of $175,000. The brokerage split with salespeople is 30/70, with 30 percent remaining with the company. How much is the salesperson's share if she both lists and sells the property?
    A. $2,625 C. $8,750
    B. $6,125 D. none of the above

3. It is the broker's office policy that salespeople keep 60 percent of the firm's share of any commission earned from any property they list. The salesperson listed a property that was later sold by a cooperating broker for $114,000. If the two brokers agree to split the 6.5 percent commission equally, what will the salesperson receive?
    A. $2,223 C. $3,705
    B. $2,923 D. $4,440

4. The commission on the sale of 119 South Wright was $10,875, based on a 7.5 percent commission rate. What was the final selling price of 119 South Wright?
    A. $81,563 C. $117,560
    B. $100,875 D. $145,000

5. The broker listed a home for $111,250 under a 90-day exclusive-right-to-sell listing agreement with a 6 percent commission. The next week, the broker began advertising the home in a local paper and showed the property to two prospective buyers. Later that week, the seller announced that he had decided to sell his home to a relative for $95,000. The seller is liable to the broker for
    A. $975 C. $6,675
    B. $5,700 D. none of the above

Listing Worksheet

Attention to Detail Pays!

Fill in the practice listing worksheet below using the floor plan of John & Martha Rambler's property shown on the opposite page. The scale is 1 inch = 12 feet (Approximate dimensions are acceptable). The property is a stuccoed, 20-year-old ranch-style house with terra cotta roof and no basement. Last year's taxes were $1,875. The original carpeting throughout is quite worn, but the tile baths are in excellent condition. A security system and TV cabling were installed in 1985. The kitchen was remodeled in 1996 with new dishwasher, range, refrigerator, compactor, disposal and vinyl floor covering.

Property Address: ______________________________ Lot Size: ____________

Owners: ______________________________ Taxes: ____________

Style ____________
Sq. Ft. ____________
Bedrooms ____________
Age ____________
Stories ____________
Basement: ____________
Garage ____________

Utilities
Elec. ____________
Heat ____________
A/C ____________
Humidifier ____________
Air Filter ____________
Water ____________

Softener ____________
Sewer ____________

Exterior
Roof ____________
Siding ____________
Deck ____________
Patio ____________

Sunroom ____________
Pool ____________
Shed ____________
Fence ____________
Landscaping ____________
Other ____________
____

Rooms	Level	Size	Floor Cover	Features	Comments
Living Room		x			
Dining Room		x			
Family Room		x			
Kitchen		x			
Rec. Room		x			
Master BR		x			
Bedroom 1		x			
Bedroom 2		x			
Bedroom 3		x			
Bath (full)		x			
Bath (3/4)		x			
Bath (1/2)		x			
Other		x			
		x			

John & Martha Rambler

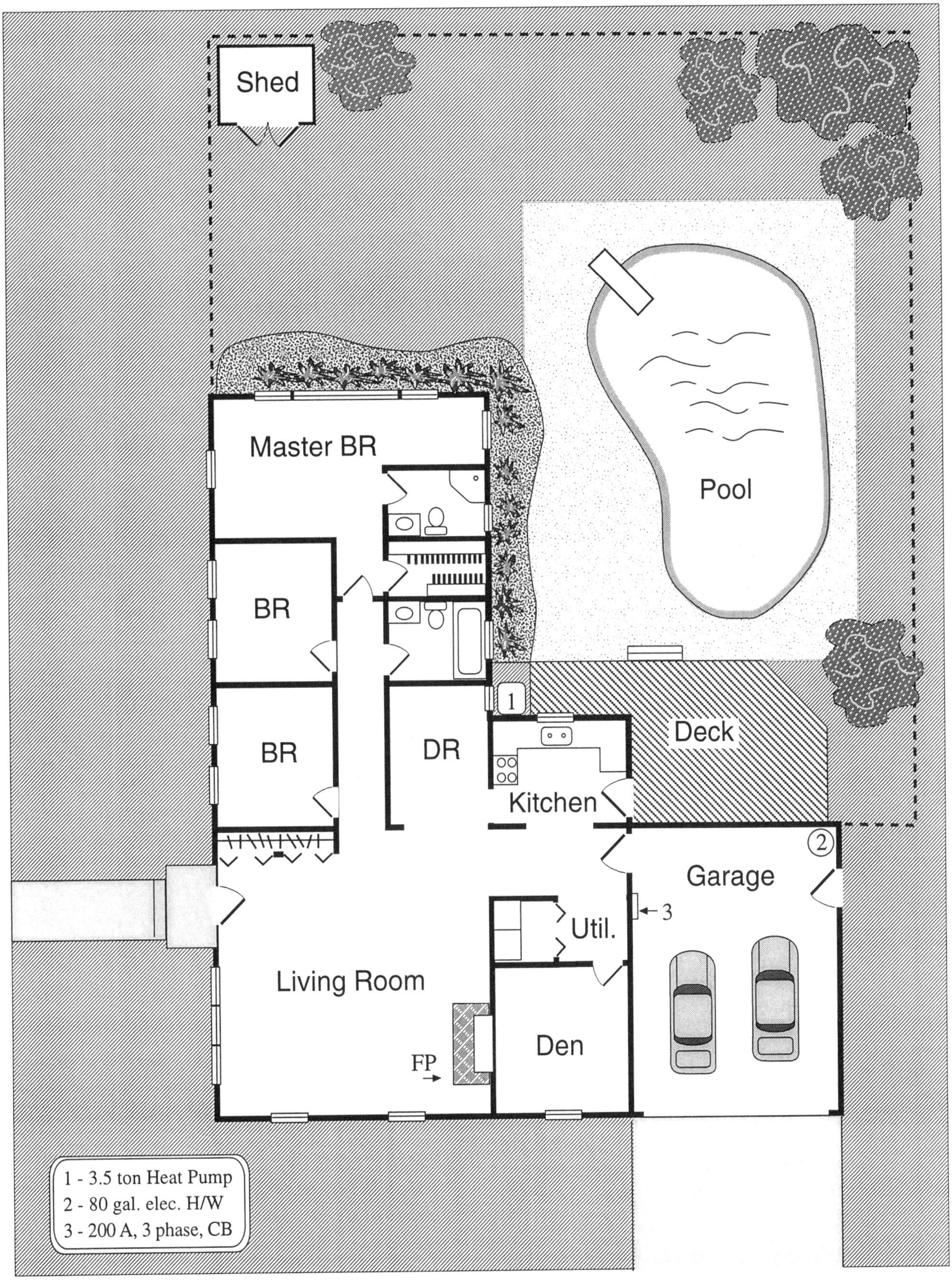

Answer Key

MATCHING ANSWERS

1. listing agreement
2. exclusive-right-to-sell listing
3. exclusive-agency listing
4. open listing
5. MLS (multiple-listing service)
6. net listing
7. CMA (competitive market analysis)
8. open buyer agency
9. exclusive buyer agency
10. option listing

TRUE OR FALSE

1. False Under a typical net listing, the broker's commission is based on the amount by which the sales price exceeds the seller's required net. There is a potential for a conflict of interest between the broker's fiduciary responsibility to the seller and the broker's profit motive.

2. False A listing agreement is an employment contract, not a contract for the sale of real estate.

3. False The parties to a listing agreement are a broker and a seller.

4. False The salesperson helps the seller set the listing price for a property by using a competitive market analysis.

5. False A listing agreement in which the seller retains the right to employ any number of brokers as agent is referred to as an open listing.

6. True

7. False In buyer agency, the source of compensation is not the major factor that determines the relationship. Who does the hiring determines the relationship.

8. True

9. False

10. False Because a listing agreement is a personal service contract between a broker and seller, the broker may not transfer the listing to another broker without the seller's written consent.

LISTING CONTRACTS

1. open listing
2. exclusive agency
3. exclusive right to sell

MULTIPLE CHOICE ANSWERS

1. A The buyer hires the agency in a buyer agency agreement; therefore the buyer is the principal/client.

2. D Of the answers given, only the open listing clearly permits the seller to sell the house and not be obligated to pay a commission.

3. C When taking the listing from the seller, the agent is not concerned at the moment what the seller's future housing needs are. A, B, and D are relevant to the listing.

4. C Some broker's delegate the responsibility for signing the listing agreement to the salesperson, but since this company has a policy of having the broker sign the listing, it does not become effective until the broker signs it – January 18.

5. C The asking price as well as the acceptance of the final offer price from the buyer is always the seller's decision. This is another example of the broker being a special agent (one with limited authority).

6. D The broker can "sub" out the work to salespeople, but the listing agreement is an employment contract between the seller and the broker.

7. B The seller and broker are parties to the listing agreement. Listings remain the property of the broker even if the salesperson leaves the company.

Continued p-46

Answer Key (Listing Worksheet)

The answers below were derived from the floor plan and information included in the narrative. The room dimensions are approximate, and were determined by measuring the floor plan with a ruler. Keep in mind that garages are not considered living space, thus are not included in the house square footage. The lot size was measured as 84' x 105' (8,820 sf) and converted to acres (8,820 ÷ 43,560 = .20 acres). The electrical and heating system specifications presume some familiarity with these technical aspects of the floor plan.

Property Address: 128 Winding Way Lot Size: 1/5 Acre

Owners: John & Martha Rambler Taxes: ______

Style: *Ranch*
Sq. Ft.: *1,850*
Bedrooms: *3*
Age: *20*
Stories: *1*
Basement: *none*
Garage: *2-car attached*

Utilities
Elec.: *200 amp, cir brkr*
Heat: *3.5 ton heat pump*
A/C: *3.5 ton heat pump*
Humidifier: *???*
Air Filter: *???*
Water: *80 gal. elec h/w*

Softener: *???*
Sewer: *???*

Exterior
Roof: *terra cotta*
Siding: *stucco*
Deck: *yes - 14 x 18 +*
Patio: *yes - around pool*

Sunroom: *none*
Pool: *yes*
Shed: *yes*
Fence: *yes*
Landscaping: *in rear*
Other: ______

Rooms	Level	Size	Floor Cover	Features	Comments
Living Room	1	24 x 24	carpet	fireplace, closet	carpet worn
Dining Room	1	9 x 12	carpet		
Family Room	-	-	---		
Kitchen	1	9 x 12	vinyl	modernized 1996	
Rec. Room	-	-	---		
Master BR	1	12 x 24 L	carpet	walk-in closet	
Bedroom 1	1	10 x 12	carpet		
Bedroom 2	1	10 x 12	carpet		
Bedroom 3	-	-	---		
Bath (full)	1	6 x 9	tile		
Bath (3/4)	1	6 x 9	tile		
Bath (1/2)	-	-	---		
Other *(Den)*	1	12 x 12	carpet		
Utility Rm	1	6 x 8	???	has washer & dryer	

Answer Key (Continued)

8. D In an open listing, the seller retains the right to sell the property and does not designate even one agent to represent the seller.

9. A Often sellers are confused thinking that the only way to find buyers from a number of brokers is to enter into an open listing. Explaining the advantages of the multiple listing service can overcome the misconception.

10. B If taking a net listing, the broker may not tell the seller the true value of the property in order to receive a higher commission. This is why net listings are generally illegal.

11. A The exclusive buyer agency agreement is the counterpart to the exclusive right to sell listing agreement. Even if the buyer finds the property on his or her own, the buyer is responsible for paying the brokerage fee.

12. D Commissions are never calculated on the listing price, only on the selling price.

13. D What the buyer paid for his or her current home is not relevant to the purchase of a new property.

14. C An offer to purchase is like the bird in the bush. It may not be accepted so therefore an offer does not terminate the listing agreement.

15. D Since the listing agreement is a contract for the personal services of the original broker, the sellers have the right to cancel their listing agreements and not go to the new broker.

MATH PRACTICE ANSWERS

1. D The sales price is $129,350 x 4% + $1,000 = $6,174 (none of the above)

2. B $175,000 x 5% x 70% = $6,125

3. A $114,000 x 6.5% x 50% x 60% = $2,223

4. D $10,875 ÷ 7.5% = $145,000

5. B $95,000 x 6% = $5,700 Since the seller had signed an exclusive right to sell listing agreement, the seller is responsible for paying a commission no matter who finds the buyer.

Interests in Real Estate

7

Matching (A)

Write the matching term on the appropriate line.

- condemnation
- defeasible fee
- eminent domain
- escheat
- estate in land
- fee simple absolute
- freehold estates
- leasehold estates
- police power
- taxation

1. ________________ A state's ability to enact legislation to preserve order, protect the public health and safety and promote the general welfare
2. ________________ The right of a government to acquire privately owned real estate for public use
3. ________________ The process by which the government exercises its right of eminent domain
4. ________________ A charge imposed on real estate to raise funding for government services
5. ________________ The automatic transfer of real property to the state when the owner dies without heirs or a will
6. ________________ The degree, quantity, nature and extent of an owner's interest in real property
7. ________________ A class of estates that last for an indeterminable period of time
8. ________________ A class of estates that last for a fixed period of time
9. ________________ The highest interest in real estate recognized by law
10. ________________ An estate qualified by some action or activity that must not be performed

True or False

Circle the answer

1. T F A state's power to enact legislation that preserves order, protects the public health and safety and promotes the general welfare is referred to as its police power.
2. T F The four governmental powers that affect real estate are taxation, eminent domain, escheat and police.
3. T F The process by which the government exercises its right to acquire privately owned real estate for public use through either judicial or administrative proceedings is called condemnation.
4. T F The purpose of escheat is to expand governmental property holdings.

True or False (Continued)

5. T F A freehold estate is the highest interest in real estate recognized by law.

6. T F Riparian rights are common-law rights granted to owners of land that lie along the course of a river, stream or similar body of water.

7. T F If the grantor is silent about what happens to property after a life estate ends, the grantor has a remainder interest in the property.

8. T F A homestead is a legal life estate in real estate occupied as a family home.

9. T F An appurtenant easement is said to run with the land, and transfers with the deed of the servient tenement.

10. T F An easement that arises when an owner sells property that has no access to a street or public way except across the seller's remaining land is an easement by prescription.

11. T F The concept of "tacking" provides that successive periods of continuous occupation by different parties may be combined to reach the required total number of years necessary to establish a claim for an easement in gross.

12. T F A license may be terminated or canceled by the person who granted it, and ends on the death of either party or the sale of the affected property by the licensor.

13. T F A conventional life estate may be created either by deed during the owner's life or after the owner's death by will.

14. T F Riparian and littoral rights are personal rights under the common law: they belong to the landowner, and do not run with the land.

15. T F To secure water rights in a state in which the doctrine of prior appropriation is in effect, landowners must demonstrate that they plan a beneficial use for the water.

Compound Interests in Spindley Acres

Based on the narrative below, enter the name of each player in the Spindley Acres scenario into the appropriate box. Also label his or her interest in the estate and how it is conveyed from one to another.

Ben conveys a life estate in Spindley Acres to Carol, with a remainder to Bob, "so long as Spindley Acres continues to be a working farm." If it ceases to be a farm, the property will go back to Ben (or his estate).

Meanwhile, Carol conveys a life estate in Spindly Acres to Sally, "for as long as my Cousin Tom shall live." When Tom dies, the estate will return to Carol for the remainder of her life.

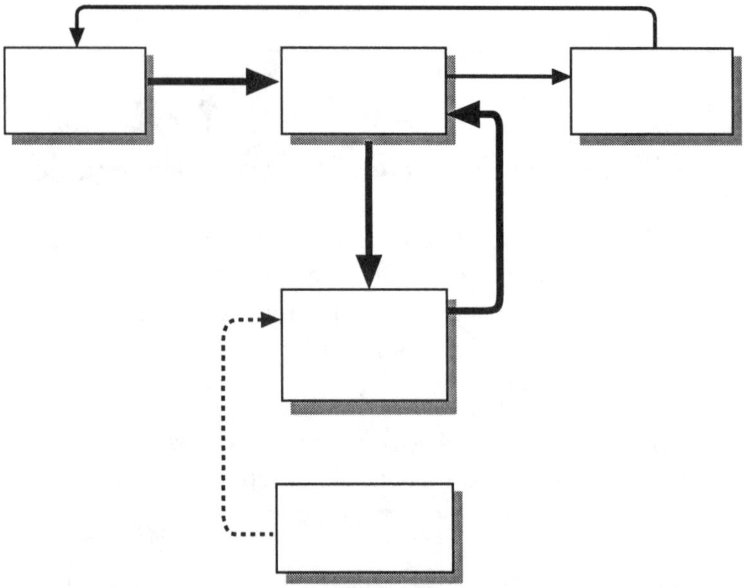

Flash Cards (Pull out page & cut with scissors)

appurtenant easement	government powers (4)
defeasible fee	leasehold estate
easement by prescription	legal life estates (3)
easement in gross	lien
encumbrance claim	reversion/remainder interests
fee simple absolute	riparian rights

Police powers, eminent domain, taxation, escheat

Chapter 7

Easement that is attached to and travels with the ownership of one parcel allowing the owner the use of the neighbor's land

Chapter 7

Tenant's right to occupy real estate during the term of a lease, generally considered to be a personal property interest

Chapter 7

Fee simple estate in which the holder may lose title if a certain event occurs or doesn't occur: "so long as...," or "no alcohol sales," etc.

Chapter 7

Curtesy (husband's rights), dower (wife's interest), homestead (protect family home from certain creditors)

Chapter 7

Easement; claimant has used another's land for a certain period of time (10-20 years) openly, continuously and without the owner's approval

Chapter 7

Monetary interest in real property; examples are mortgage liens, mechanics liens

Chapter 7

Individual interest in someone else's land; no dominant tenement. Commercial may be assigned, conveyed or inherited; examples: utility lines, sewer, water

Chapter 7

Future ownership rights after life estate ends: remainder interest passes to a third party; reversionary interest reverts to the original owner or heirs

Chapter 7

Charge or liability that attaches to real estate: liens, restrictions, easements, encroachments

Chapter 7

Owner's rights in land that borders on or includes a stream, river or lake. Rights include access to and use of the water.

Chapter 7

Maximum possible estate or right of ownership of real property, continuing forever

Chapter 7

Multiple Choice

Circle A, B, C or D

1. An elderly man left the family home to his second wife with the provision that when she dies, the home goes to a son by his first wife. The second wife owns a bundle of rights; however, she does not own the right to
   A. will the property.
   B. sell the property.
   C. lease the property.
   D. decorate the property.

2. Every work day for the past 20 years, J has parked her car in a specific place in the nearby parking garage. Today she receives a notice that the garage will be replaced by an office building. Can they do this to her after all the years she parked there?
   A. No, since she has been parking there for more than 20 years, she has an easement by prescription.
   B. No, since she paid regularly on time.
   C. Yes, because she only had a license.
   D. Yes, because she has nothing in writing.

3. F conveyed a one-acre parcel of land to the Wee Fry Preschool. In the deed, F stated that the property was to be used only as a playground; F reserved a right of reentry. What kind of estate has F granted?
   A. Leasehold
   B. Fee simple subject to a condition subsequent
   C. Fee simple absolute
   D. Freehold

4. T owns a farm that lies along the edge of the Brackish River, which is too shallow to be navigable. If T does not live in a jurisdiction that recognizes the doctrine of prior appropriation, how much (if any) of the river does T own?
   A. T owns the land to the edge of the river; the land under the river is owned by the state.
   B. T owns the land to the mean high water mark, and a right to apply for a water use permit.
   C. T owns the land up to the water's edge and the right to use the water.
   D. T owns the land under the river to the exact center of the waterway, and the right to use the water.

5. Over the past 15 years, the Brackish River has been slowly depositing soil along its eastern bank. As a result, the river is some 12 feet narrower than it used to be, and Rambling Acres, the property on the east side of the river, is now 12 feet larger than it used to be. This scenario is an example of which of the following processes?
   A. Reliction
   B. Erosion
   C. Alluvion
   D. Accretion

6. If the government acquires privately owned real estate through a condemnation suit, it is exercising its power of
   A. escheat.
   B. reverter.
   C. eminent domain.
   D. defeasance.

7. L owned two acres. L sold one acre to Q and reserved an easement appurtenant for entrance and exit over Q's acre to reach the public road. Q's land
   A. can be cleared of the easement if Q sells to a third party.
   B. is called the servient tenement.
   C. is called the dominant tenement.
   D. is subject to an easement in gross.

8. N owns a large island in the middle of a navigable river and a strip of land along the shore. N sells the strip on the riverbank to the Granola County Canoe Club. For N to gain access to the island, N must claim by implication of law an easement
   A. by necessity.
   B. in gross.
   C. by prescription.
   D. by restriction.

9. If the dominant estate merges with the servient estate, which of the following is true?
   A. The easement remains in effect for the entire parcel.
   B. The easement is suspended but cannot be terminated.
   C. The easement is terminated.
   D. The new owner must bring a suit seeking severance of the easement from the combined properties.

Multiple Choice (Continued)

10. In the state of New Freedonia, the homestead exemption is $15,000. Four years ago, G, a resident of New Freedonia, purchased a home for $58,500. G then fell on hard times. At a court-ordered sale, G's property is purchased for $60,000. If G has an outstanding mortgage balance of $35,000 and other debts amounting to $24,360, how much is protected by the homestead exemption?
    A. $640
    B. $2,140
    C. $15,000
    D. $16,500

11. In some states, a husband cannot sell his property unless his wife also signs the deed. His wife's interest is called
    A. common law rights.
    B. homestead rights.
    C. curtesy rights.
    D. dower rights.

12. The state's authority to enact legislation to protect the public is passed through to municipalities and counties through
    A. police power.
    B. enabling acts.
    C. licensing laws.
    D. processing papers.

13. The state requires enough land to build a four-lane highway. In order for the state to acquire the needed land, the state must do all of the following EXCEPT
    A. demonstrate that this is for the public good.
    B. pay a fair and just compensation to the owner.
    C. allow the property owner the right to appeal any decision.
    D. reimburse the farmer for the amount that the farmer paid for the land.

14. A 100-year old woman died in a nursing home. She had outlived all of her relatives and had not written a will. What happens to her $250,000 estate?
    A. Escheats to the state
    B. The nursing home gets to keep it.
    C. It will be split between the nursing home and the county.
    D. It can be paid over to her church.

15. Which of the following is a claim, charge or liability that attaches to the real estate?
    A. Lien
    B. Easement
    C. Deed restriction
    D. Encumbrance

16. Which of the following must exist for an appurtenant easement to exist?
    A. Two parcels next to each other, two different owners
    B. Two parcels next to each other, one owner
    C. Landlocked property that requires passage to the street
    D. Long time unauthorized usage

17. What are deed restrictions?
    A. Public land restrictions
    B. Illegal land restrictions
    C. Private agreements affecting the use of the land
    D. Informal agreements between neighbors

18. The electric company has the right to string its wires over 50 parcels of land. What right does the electric company possess?
    A. Appurtenant easement
    B. Easement by necessity
    C. Easement by prescription
    D. Easement in gross

19. For as long as anyone can remember, families have used a foot path along the fence to get to the river. Recently, the current owner erected a fence across the path. Which of the following easements may require that he take down the fence?
    A. Easement by necessity
    B. Easement by prescription
    C. Easement in gross
    D. Appurtenant easement

20. The rights of property owners of land next to large bodies of water, such as the ocean or the Great Lakes, are called
    A. riparian rights.
    B. littoral rights.
    C. prior appropriation.
    D. reversionary rights

Matching (B)

Write the matching term on the appropriate line.

- deed restriction
- prior appropriation
- encroachment
- encumbrance
- homestead
- easement
- life estate pur autre vie
- lien
- right of reentry
- remainderman

1. ______________ The owner's right to retake possession of property through legal action if a limiting condition is broken
2. ______________ An estate based on the lifetime of a person other than the life tenant
3. ______________ The person to whom property passes when a life estate ends
4. ______________ A legal life estate in which an individual's primary residence is protected, in whole or in part, against certain creditors
5. ______________ Any claim, charge or liability that attaches to real estate
6. ______________ A charge against property that provides security for a debt or obligation of the property owner
7. ______________ A private agreement that affects the use of land
8. ______________ The right to use another's land for a particular purpose
9. ______________ All or part of a structure that extends beyond the land of its owner or beyond legal building lines
10. ______________ The doctrine that the right to use any water, with the exception of limited domestic uses, is held and controlled by the state

Answer Key

MATCHING ANSWERS (A)

1. police power
2. eminent domain
3. condemnation
4. taxation
5. escheat
6. estate in land
7. freehold estates
8. leasehold estates
9. fee simple absolute
10. defeasible fee

TRUE OR FALSE

1. True
2. True
3. True
4. False The purpose of escheat is to prevent property from being ownerless or abandoned.
5. False A fee simple estate is the highest interest in real estate recognized by law.
6. True

Answer Key (Continued)

TRUE OR FALSE

7. False — If the grantor is silent about what happens to property after a life estate ends, the grantor has a reversionary interest in the property.
8. True
9. False — An appurtenant easement is said to run with the land, and transfers with the deed of the dominant tenement.
10. False — An easement that arises when an owner sells property that has no access to a street or public way except across the seller's remaining land is an easement by necessity.
11. False — The concept of "tacking" provides that successive periods of continuous occupation by different parties may be combined to reach the required total number of years necessary to establish a claim for an easement by prescription.
12. True
13. True
14. False — Riparian and littoral rights are attached to the land.
15. True

SPINDLEY ACRES INTERESTS

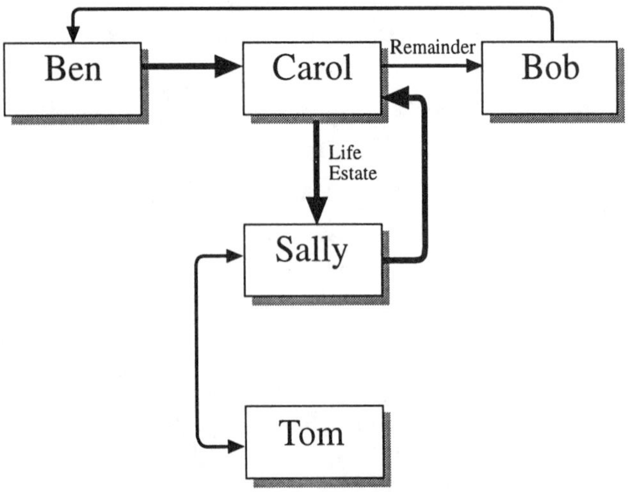

MULTIPLE CHOICE ANSWERS

1. A — The second wife owns a life estate, and she has the entire bundle of rights except the right to will the property.
2. C — A license is a personal right to enter the property for a specific purpose. There is no "build up" of rights.
3. B — F has granted a fee simple subject to a condition subsequent; that is, he reserved the right to reenter to ensure that the property is being used only as a playground.
4. D — Unless otherwise stipulated by state rules or a deed, the owner of property along a river has the right to use the water and owns the land under the water to the center of the stream.
5. D — Accretion is the increase in the land resulting from the deposit of soil by the water's action. The new deposits may be referred to as alluvion. Reliction is the resulting land when water dries up, and erosion is the slow washing away of land by natural forces.
6. C — The right of the state to acquire private property for public use is eminent domain. The court action is called condemnation. Property escheats back to the state when it becomes ownerless, that is, the owner dies intestate leaving no heirs.
7. B — L's parcel is the dominant tenement and benefits from the easement. The easement runs over Q's property, the servient tenement.
8. A — An easement by necessity is created by court order in order to permit legal access to the island.
9. C — Merger, that is, one owner with two lots, terminates the easement.
10. C — The homestead exemption is $15,000. So, when the property is sold for $60,000, the mortgage of $35,000 is paid, $15,000 is reserved, leaving $10,000 for the rest of the creditors who will be paid on priority, first recorded, first paid until the money runs out.

Answer Key (Continued)

11. D A wife's interest in her deceased husband's property is dower; a husband's interest is curtesy; protection for some part of the family home is referred to as homestead rights.

12. B The state passes police power to local counties and municipalities through enabling acts. Licensing laws are an example of police power.

13. D To acquire private property through eminent domain, the state must prove that the purchase is for public good, pay a fair price (market value), allow the property owner full rights to appeal. Market value may or may not reflect what the owner had actually paid for the property.

14. A Since the woman died intestate (no will) and there are no heirs, essentially, the $250,000 is ownerless. It reverts to the state.

15. D Encumbrances include liens, easements and deed restrictions.

16. A An easement appurtenant must have two owners, two parcels of land. A landlocked parcel would require an easement by necessity; long-time unauthorized usage would lead to an easement by prescription.

17. C Deed restrictions are private agreements written into the deed and are privately enforced. Examples of public restrictions include zoning and building codes.

18. D Commercial easements are called easements in gross. There are only servient tenements, no dominant tenement.

19. B Long-time unauthorized usage may create legal rights leading to an easement by prescription. An easement in gross is a personal right, often used by utility companies. An easement by necessity could be imposed by court order in order to free up a landlocked property.

20. B Property owners along large bodies of water have littoral rights; riparian rights are those found along rivers and streams. The doctrine of prior appropriation refers to the state controlling the right to water from the river, rather than the adjacent property owner.

MATCHING ANSWERS (B)

1. right of reentry
2. life estate pur autre vie
3. remainderman
4. homestead
5. encumbrance
6. lien
7. deed restriction
8. easement
9. encroachment
10. prior appropriation

8

Forms of Real Estate Ownership

Matching (A)

Write the matching term on the appropriate line.

- tenancy in common
- joint tenancy
- partition
- partnership
- proprietary lease
- severalty
- tenancy by the entirety
- board of directors
- trust
- testamentary trust

1. ______________ Ownership of real estate by one individual
2. ______________ A form of ownership in which each tenant holds an undivided fractional interest in the property and is inheritable by their heirs
3. ______________ A form of ownership in which multiple owners hold property with a right of survivorship
4. ______________ A legal method for dissolving a co-ownership
5. ______________ A special form of co-ownership for married couples
6. ______________ A device by which one person transfers ownership of property to someone else to hold or manage for the benefit of a third party
7. ______________ A form of trust established by will after the owner's death
8. ______________ An association of two or more persons who carry on a business for profit as co-owners
9. ______________ The evidence of possession in a cooperative
10. ______________ The governing body of a cooperative

True or False

Circle the answer

1. T F There are three basic ways in which a fee simple estate may be held: in severalty, in co-ownership and in trust.
2. T F The term "severalty" means that there is only one owner of a single property.
3. T F In a tenancy in common, title is held as though all owners collectively constitute a single common unit, with the right of survivorship.
4. T F The ownership of an undivided fractional interest in a property is characteristic of a tenancy in common.
5. T F A joint tenancy continues indefinitely, until there is only one remaining owner, who then holds title in entirety.
6. T F When title to a single parcel of real estate is held by two or more individuals, the parties may be referred to as "concurrent owners."

Flash Cards (Pull out page & cut with scissors)

community property	partnership
co-ownership	right of survivorship
corporation	severalty
4 unities of joint tenancy	tenancy in common
joint tenancy	time sharing
partition	trust

Under law, a group of individuals who carry on a continuing business for profit as co-owners; regarded as a single entity

Chapter 8

System of ownership: each spouse has an equal interest in property acquired during marriage; separate property is that acquired before marriage

Chapter 8

When a joint tenant dies, his or her interest passes to the remaining owners of the property; becomes an issue only at death of one of the owners

Chapter 8

Title ownership held by two or more persons who must agree on how the property is used.

Chapter 8

Ownership of real estate by one person only, although a corporation (single entity) can own in severalty

Chapter 8

An artificial entity created by operation of law whose rights in business are similar to those of an individual. Continuous existence until it is legally dissolved

Chapter 8

Form of co-ownership in which each owner holds an undivided interest as if he or she were sole owners; individual owners have right to partition, right of inheritance

Chapter 8

PITT: Possession, Interest, Time and Title. All four must exist simultaneously for joint tenancy to exist

Chapter 8

Form of ownership that allows use of the property for a fixed or variable time frame, often used in resorts

Chapter 8

Co-ownership of real estate; when one of the owners dies, that interest goes to the remaining owners
(right of survivorship)

Chapter 8

Fiduciary arrangement whereby the owner (trustor) conveys property to a third party, (trustee), to be held and administered on behalf of another person (beneficiary)

Chapter 8

Court procedure dividing up cotenants' interest in real property when the parties do not all voluntarily agree to terminate the co-ownership

Chapter 8

True or False (Continued)

7. T F The four unities characteristic of a tenancy in common are possession, interest, title and time.

8. T F A joint tenant may freely convey his or her interest in the jointly held property to a new owner, who becomes a joint tenant.

9. T F A cotenancy may be terminated by asking a court to partition the property.

10. T F A tenancy by the entirety is a special form of ownership limited to married couples, neither can convey a half-interest, no right to partition or divide the property.

11. T F A tenancy by the entirety may be terminated only by divorce or death.

12. T F In a community property state, "community property" includes all property, both real and personal, acquired by either party prior to or during the marriage.

13. T F The person who creates a trust is referred to as the "trustor."

14. T F In a limited partnership, the death of one of the officers does not affect the organization's continuity.

15. T F When a corporation buys real property, the stockholders have a direct ownership interest in the real estate that is proportional to their stock interest.

16. T F A syndicate is a form of partnership in which two or more people or firms carry out a single business project, with no intention of establishing an ongoing or permanent relationship.

17. T F Condominium owners hold their own units in fee simple and the common elements under proprietary leases.

18. T F The management and operation of a cooperative are determined by the bylaws of the corporation that owns the property.

19. T F Ownership of a cooperative interest is personal property.

20. T F A time-share estate is the right to use the property for a certain period of time.

Types of Ownership

Check the characteristics that apply to the type of ownership assigned to each building.

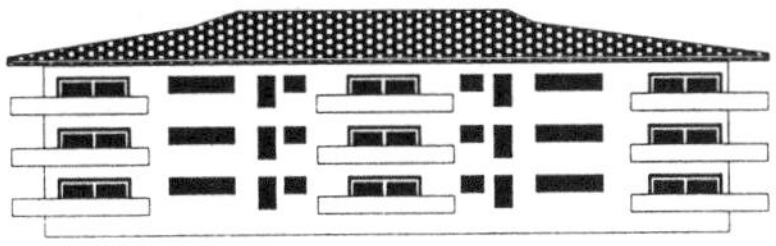

Condominium

- ❑ corporate ownership
- ❑ undivided interest in common elements
- ❑ occupancy and use for limited periods
- ❑ proprietary lease
- ❑ fee simple ownerhip of units

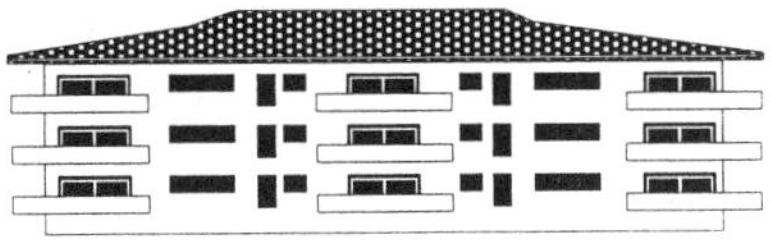

Cooperative

- ❑ corporate ownership
- ❑ undivided interest in common elements
- ❑ occupancy and use for limited periods
- ❑ proprietary lease
- ❑ fee simple ownerhip of units

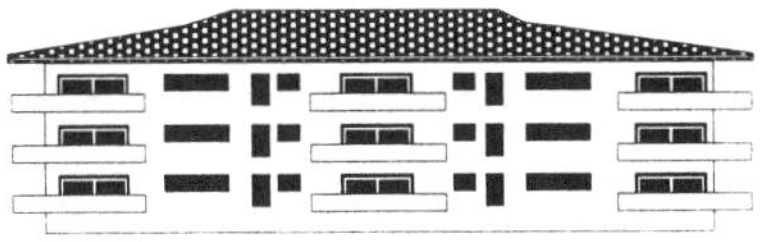

Time Share

- ❑ corporate ownership
- ❑ undivided interest in common elements
- ❑ occupancy and use for limited periods
- ❑ proprietary lease
- ❑ fee simple ownerhip of units

Matching (B)

Write the matching term on the appropriate line.

- assessments
- condo fee
- condominium
- corporation
- general partnership
- joint venture
- limited liability company
- separate property
- time-share estate
- time-share use

1. ______________ A business organization in which all members participate in the operation and management of the business and share full liability for business losses and obligations
2. ______________ A business organization that is a legal entity managed and operated by a board of directors
3. ______________ A business organization in which two or more people or firms carry out a single business project
4. ______________ A business organization that combines features of limited partnerships and corporations
5. ______________ In a community property state, real or personal property that was owned solely by either spouse prior to marriage or acquired by inheritance during the marriage
6. ______________ A form of property ownership in which each owner holds an undivided interest in certain common elements in addition to holding his or her own property in fee simple
7. ______________ Special payments required of condominium unit owners to address specific expenses
8. ______________ Recurring fees required of condominium unit owners to cover basic maintenance and operations
9. ______________ A fee simple interest in a property that entitles the owner to use the facility for a certain period of time
10. ______________ A contract right under which a developer retains ownership of property and the purchaser receives the right to occupy and use the facilities for a certain period

Multiple Choice

Circle A, B, C or D

1. Which of the following may never take title as a joint tenancy with right of survivorship?
   A. Wife and husband
   B. Two female business partners
   C. Two brothers in partnership
   D. Corporation

2. When two or more individuals decide to buy a property together, it is called
   A. cooperation.
   B. co-ownership.
   C. community effort.
   D. joint venture.

Multiple Choice (Continued)

3. Three brothers bought a farm together. The deed listed only each of their names. What form of ownership are they presumed to have taken?
   A. Tenancy by the entireties
   B. Joint tenancy with right of survivorship
   C. Tenancy in common
   D. In severalty

4. What form of ownership is employed when one person transfers ownership to someone else to hold and manage for yet another third person?
   A. Joint venture C. Trust
   B. Joint tenancy D. Severalty

5. A man with two sons and a woman with two daughters are getting married and buying a house together. They ask the real estate licensee for advice on how to take title. What advice should the licensee offer?
   A. Tenants in common, so that each one-half interest would go to the appropriate children
   B. Joint tenancy to protect so that if one dies, the other gets the house
   C. Suggest that they consult with the employing broker
   D. Suggest that they consult with an attorney

6. The will provided that the local banker take care of the deceased person's estate until the children turned 25. What kind of trust is this?
   A. Testamentary trust C. Land trust
   B. Living trust D. Trust deed

7. What kind of ownership do the horizontal property acts regulate?
   A. Cooperatives
   B. Condominiums
   C. Timesharing
   D. Planned unit developments

8. Shareholders in a cooperative receive a share of stock that is inseparable from the
   A. common elements. C. proprietary lease.
   B. trust deed. D. corporate deed.

9. Membership camping is similar to
   A. cooperative ownership.
   B. condominium ownership.
   C. planned use development.
   D. time sharing.

10. In a large high-rise building, each unit is owned by individual owners. The elevators, parking garage and swimming pool are referred to as
    A. community property.
    B. separate property
    C. common elements.
    D. proprietary elements.

11. P and J own an apartment building together as joint tenants. They share equally in the expenses and profits. One day, P decides to end the relationship. If P sells her interest to K by signing and delivering a deed, which of the following statements is true?
    A. K will become a joint tenant with J.
    B. K and J will be tenants in common.
    C. K will be a tenant in common with J and a joint tenant with P.
    D. The conveyance will be invalid: P and J will remain joint tenants.

12. In February, G conveyed an undivided one-half interest in Sunny Orchard to Q. In March, G conveyed the remaining one-half interest to R. The deed to R included the following statement: "R is to be a joint tenant with Q." Both deeds were recorded. Based on these facts, which of the following statements is true?
    A. Q and R hold title to Sunny Orchard as joint tenants under the terms of the two conveyances from G.
    B. Q and R own Sunny Orchard by partition.
    C. Q and R are tenants in common.
    D. R owns Sunny Orchard as a joint tenant; Q owns Sunny Orchard as a tenant in common.

13. E, F and G own a large parcel of undeveloped land in joint tenancy. E wants to build a shopping center on the property, while F and G want to use it as an organic farm. E tries to buy the other tenant's interests, but they refuse. Which of the following is E's best option?
    A. File a suit for partition
    B. Begin building a shopping center on one-third of the property
    C. Wait for F and G to die
    D. File a suit to quiet title

Multiple Choice (Continued)

14. T owns a cottage in the Walden Acres community on the shore of Loon Lake. T's ownership of the cottage is in fee simple. T also owns an undivided percentage interest in a parking lot, a golf course and a swimming pool, all located in the Walden Acres development. Based on these facts alone, T's ownership is probably best described as a
    A. time-share estate.
    B. time-share use.
    C. condominium.
    D. cooperative.

15. P, Q and R agree to purchase and operate Rickety Tower as a permanent investment. P and Q each contribute $50,000. R contributes $30,000 and agrees to run the day-to-day operations of the business, which they call "Rickety Tower Joint Venture Partners." Neither P nor Q has any right to participate in the operation of the venture. Based on these facts, what type of business organization have P, Q and R established?
    A. Joint venture
    B. Limited partnership
    C. General partnership
    D. Limited liability company

16. Based on the facts in the previous question, if Rickety Tower collapses, resulting in injury and property damage worth $275,000, what will be P's liability?
    A. None
    B. $50,000
    C. $91,667
    D. $100,000

17. All of the following are unities required for a joint tenancy EXCEPT
    A. unity of title.
    B. unity of ownership.
    C. unity of time.
    D. unity of possession.

18. All of the following are characteristics of a tenancy by the entirety EXCEPT
    A. title may be conveyed only by a deed signed by both parties.
    B. the surviving spouse automatically becomes sole owner of the property upon the death of the other spouse.
    C. each spouse owns an equal, undivided interest in the property as a single, indivisible unit.
    D. the surviving spouse automatically owns one-half of the property acquired during the marriage.

19. N creates a trust to pay for M's real estate education. The trust is operated by O, who makes payments on M's behalf directly to The Real Estate School. Based on these facts, which of the following statements best characterizes the relationships among these parties?
    A. N is the trustee, M is the beneficiary and O is the trustor.
    B. N is the trustor, O is the trustee and The Real Estate School is the beneficiary.
    C. N is the trustor, M is the beneficiary and O is the trustee.
    D. N is the trustor, M is the beneficiary, O is the trustee and The Real Estate School is the fiduciary.

20. XYZ is a legal entity, created by charter under the laws of the state of East Carolina. XYZ is managed and operated by a board and is permitted to buy and sell real estate. When one of its directors dies, XYZ continues to operate. Because of its structure, XYZ's income is subject to double taxation. XYZ is best described as a(n)
    A. partnership.
    B. S corporation.
    C. corporation.
    D. limited liability company.

Answer Key

MATCHING ANSWERS (A)

1. severalty
2. tenancy in common
3. joint tenancy
4. partition
5. tenancy by the entirety
6. trust
7. testamentary trust
8. partnership
9. proprietary lease
10. board of directors

TRUE OR FALSE

1. True
2. True
3. False In a **joint tenancy**, title is held as though all owners collectively constitute a single common unit, with the right of survivorship.
4. True
5. False A joint tenancy continues indefinitely, until there is only one remaining owner, who then holds title in severalty.
6. True
7. False The four unities characteristic of a joint tenancy are possession, interest, title and time.
8. False A joint tenant may freely convey his or her interest in the jointly held property to a new owner, but doing so will destroy the unities of time and title and the new owner cannot become a joint tenant.
9. True
10. True
11. False A tenancy by the entirety may be terminated by divorce, agreement, court order or the death of one of the parties.
12. False In a community property state, "community property" includes all property, both real and personal, acquired by either party during the marriage.
13. True
14. True
15. False When a corporation buys real property, the stockholders do not have a direct ownership interest in the real estate because stock is personal property.
16. False A joint venture is a form of partnership in which two or more people or firms carry out a single business project, with no intention of establishing an on-going or permanent relationship.
17. False Condominium owners hold their own units in fee simple, and the common elements as tenants in common.
18. True
19. True
20. True

TYPES OF OWNERSHIP

Condominium
- ✓ undivided interest in common elements
- ✓ fee simple ownerhip of units

Cooperative
- ✓ corporate ownership
- ✓ occupancy and use for limited periods
- ✓ proprietary lease

Time-Share
- ✓ undivided interest in common elements
- ✓ occupancy and use for limited periods
- ✓ fee simple ownerhip of units

MATCHING ANSWERS (B)

1. general partnership
2. corporation
3. joint venture
4. limited liability company
5. separate property
6. condominium

Answer Key (Continued)

7. assessments
8. condo fee
9. time-share estate
10. time-share use

MULTIPLE CHOICE ANSWERS

1. D Since a corporation continues indefinitely until terminated by legal action, a corporation may never take title as a joint tenant. It would never die.

2. B When two or more people buy property together, it is called co-ownership. A joint venture is a form of partnership in which two or more people carry out a single business project with no intention of establishing an ongoing relationship.

3. C The brothers are presumed to be tenants in common inasmuch as they did not indicate "as joint tenants with right of survivorship." Joint tenancy requires extra wording; it is sometimes called the "poor man's will." Severalty ownership indicates one owner.

4. C Severalty indicates one owner. A joint venture is a form of partnership. Joint tenancy is a form of ownership whereby the surviving owners increase their share of the property when an owner dies.

5. D The only possible answer here is to refer the couple to an attorney. Real estate licensees and their brokers are not permitted to give legal advice.

6. A A testamentary trust is established after a death. A living trust is established during the lifetime. Real estate is the only asset in a land trust. Trust deed is an inaccurate term and should not be used.

7. B Condominiums are regulated by the horizontal property acts enacted in most states.

8. C Common elements refer to the property owned jointly by condominium owners. The proprietary lease is part of the cooperative stock and gives the owner the right to a specific apartment.

9. D The owner of membership camping purchases the right to use the developer's facilities; the owner may not be limited to a specific time as in the case of a typical time share arrangement.

10. C The property that condominium owners own together is referred to as common elements. Community property is a system of property ownership based on the theory that each spouse has an equal interest in property acquired during the marriage, making a distinction from property acquire before marriage, that is, separate property.

11. B A co-owner can sell what he or she owns. However, once the unities of time, title and interest are destroyed, as they are when P sells her interest to K, there can no longer be a joint tenancy.

12. C Since there are two deeds, made at different times, the four unities of joint tenancy have not been met. Therefore, Q and R are tenants in common.

13. A When co-owners cannot come to an agreement, they must file for partition in court. The property will not physically be divided; rather, one or more will be given the opportunity to buy the others out. If this is not possible, then the property will be sold, and the money divided appropriately.

14. C It appears that T has condominium ownership since he owns the cottage as well as an interest in the common elements. Cooperative ownership is ruled out since he does not have a proprietary lease. It is not a time share since he clearly owns more than the right to use at specific times.

15. B A limited partnership limits the participation of the silent partners as well as limiting their liability. A general partnership would require that all are equally involved in running the operation and all are exposed to liability.

16. B A limited partner is limited in liability to the amount of his or her investment, in this case, $50,000.

Answer Key (Continued)

17. B There is no such thing as unity of ownership. The missing unity is that of interest.

18. D A, B, and C are all true statements about tenancy by the entirety. D is a summary of community property.

19. C N is the owner/trustor; M is the beneficiary; O is the person who manages the trust, that is, the trustee.

20. C Both the S corporation and corporation would not be affected if one of the directors dies. The tip off to this answer is "double taxation." The S corporation was created to avoid the double taxation imposed on a corporation.

9 Legal Descriptions

Matching

Write the matching term on the appropriate line.

- metes-and-bounds
- rectangular survey system
- correction lines
- monuments
- lot-and-block
- benchmarks
- datum
- POB
- township lines
- range lines

1. ______________ The type of legal description that relies on a property's physical features to describe and determine the boundaries and measurements of the parcel
2. ______________ The designated starting point for a metes-and-bounds description
3. ______________ Fixed objects used to identify significant points of measurement in a metes-and-bounds description
4. ______________ A land description system based on principal meridians and base lines
5. ______________ Lines running six miles apart and parallel to the base line
6. ______________ Strips of land running parallel to the meridian
7. ______________ A device to compensate for inaccurate measurements and the shape of the earth
8. ______________ A system of description that uses numbers referred to in a plat map
9. ______________ A point, line or surface from which elevations are measured
10. ______________ Permanent reference markers, usually found on embossed brass markers set in concrete or asphalt

True or False

Circle the answer

1. T F The metes-and-bounds description was established by Congress in 1785.
2. T F In the metes-and-bounds system, a monument may be either a natural object or a manmade marker.
3. T F Principal meridians run east and west.
4. T F Township lines and base lines are parallel.
5. T F Ranges are strips of land six miles wide that run parallel to the base line.
6. T F When the horizontal township lines and the vertical range lines intersect, they form township squares.

True or False (Continued)

7. T F Every township contains 36 sections of 640 acres each.

8. T F A datum is a permanent reference point, usually found on an embossed brass marker set into a solid concrete or asphalt base.

9. T F Section 6 is always in the northeast or upper left-hand corner.

10. T F Air lots are composed of the airspace within specific boundaries located over a parcel of land.

Multiple Choice

Circle A, B, C or D

1. Which of the following most accurately describes a quarter section?
   A. 1/4 mile by 1/4 mile
   B. 1/2 mile by 1/2 mile
   C. 1/2 mile by 1 mile
   D. 1/8 mile by 1/8 mile

2. How many acres are contained in a parcel described as follows: The NE 1/4 of the NW 1/4; the N 1/2 of the NW 1/4, NE 1/4, Section 10?
   A. 40 acres
   B. 60 acres
   C. 70 acres
   D. 74 acres

3. K sells six acres of prime undeveloped property to L for $2.25 per square foot. How much did L pay?
   A. $466,560
   B. $588,060
   C. $612,360
   D. $733,860

4. Which township section number is directly north of Section 7?
   A. Section 1
   B. Section 6
   C. Section 5
   D. Section 8

5. All of the following are used to express a legal description EXCEPT
   A. lot-and-block.
   B. metes-and-bounds.
   C. rectangular survey system.
   D. benchmarks.

6. The end of a metes-and-bounds land description is always a
   A. monument.
   B. benchmark.
   C. point of beginning.
   D. base line.

7. Years ago, a farm was typically a quarter section. How many acres is that?
   A. 20 acres
   B. 80 acres
   C. 160 acres
   D. 320 acres

8. Air lots, condominium descriptions and other vertical measurements may be computed from the U.S. Geological Survey
   A. datum.
   B. benchmark.
   C. principal meridian.
   D. base line.

9. A farmer is willing to pay $1,200 per acre. He is planning to buy the SE 1/4 of the SE 1/4 of the SE 1/4 of Section II. How much will he pay for the land?
   A. $3,000
   B. $6,000
   C. $12,000
   D. $24,000

Figure 9.1

Multiple Choice (Continued)

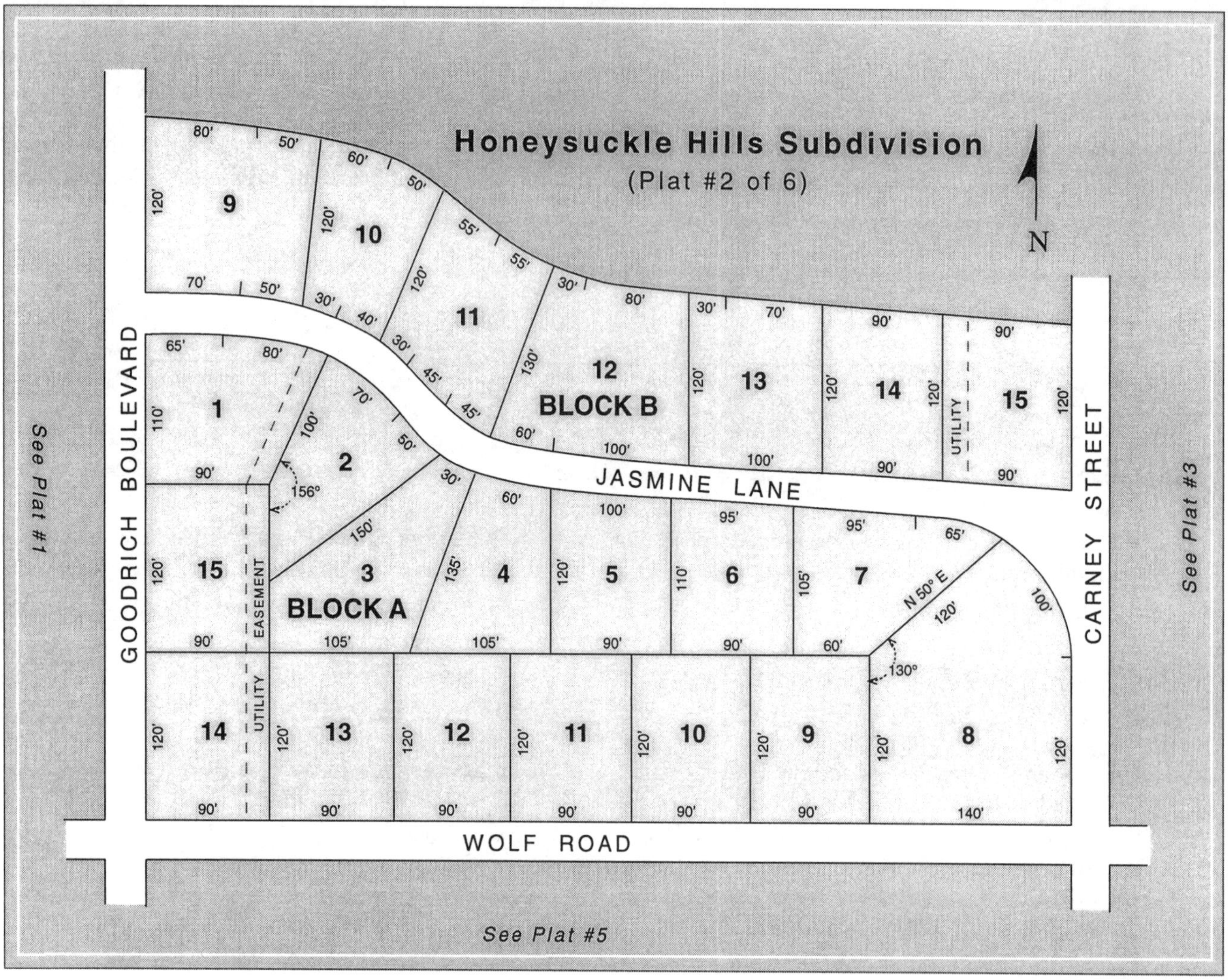

Refer to the above plat for questions 10 through 15.

10. Which lot in Block A has the most frontage on Jasmine Lane?
    A. 1
    B. 2
    C. 7
    D. 11

11. How many lots have easements?
    A. 1
    B. 3
    C. 4
    D. 6

12. Which road or roads run east and west?
    A. Wolf and Jasmine
    B. Carney and Goodrich
    C. Wolf only
    D. Goodrich only

13. Which lot has the least street exposure?
    A. Lot 3, Block A
    B. Lot 15, Block B
    C. Lot 9, Block A
    D. Lot 10, Block B

14. Beginning at the intersection of the West line of Carney Street and the North line of Wolf Road, running west 140 feet, then North 120 feet, then North 50 degrees East 120 feet, then following the southeasterly curvature of the South line of Jasmine Lane for 100 feet, then South 120 feet to POB.

    To which lot does this description refer?
    A. Lot 15, Block B
    B. Lot 8, Block A
    C. Lots 7, 8 and 9, Block A
    D. Lots 8 and 9, Block A

15. If lots 13 and 14, Block A were combined into one parcel, how many square feet would it contain?
    A. 1,020
    B. 19,800
    C. 22,800
    D. 21,600

Flash Cards (Pull out page & cut with scissors)

air lot	metes-and-bounds
base line	monuments
benchmark	plat map
datum	point of beginning
legal description	ranges
lot-and-block (recorded plat)	rectangular survey system

Legal description that begins at a well-marked point and follows the boundaries around the tract, back to the place of beginning

Chapter 9

Designated airspace over a piece of land; may be transferred; used in describing a condominium unit

Chapter 9

Fixed natural or artificial object used to establish real estate boundaries for a metes-and-bounds description

Chapter 9

Imaginary line running east and west used by surveyors as a reference in describing land under the rectangular survey system

Chapter 9

Map of a town, section or subdivision indicating the location and boundaries of individual properties

Chapter 9

Permanent reference mark of point established for use by surveyors in measuring differences in elevation

Chapter 9

The starting point in a metes-and-bounds legal description; these descriptions must follow the boundaries back to the point of beginning

Chapter 9

Horizontal plane from which heights and depths are measured

Chapter 9

Strip of land six miles wide in rectangular survey system of land description, going north and south and numbered according to its distance from the principal meridian

Chapter 9

Description of a specific parcel of real estate complete enough for an independent surveyor to locate and identify it

Chapter 9

System for surveying and describing land by reference to principal meridians and base lines; also called government survey system

Chapter 9

Method of describing property that identifies a parcel of land by reference to lot-and-block numbers within a subdivision, as specified on a recorded subdivision plat

Chapter 9

Answer Key

MATCHING

1. metes and bounds
2. POB (point of beginning)
3. monuments
4. rectangular survey system
5. township lines
6. range lines
7. correction lines
8. lot-and-block
9. datum
10. benchmarks

TRUE OR FALSE

1. False The rectangular survey system was established by Congress in 1785.
2. True
3. False Principal meridians run north and south.
4. True
5. False Range lines are strips of land six miles wide that run parallel to the meridian.
6. True
7. True
8. False A benchmark is a permanent reference point, usually found on an embossed brass marker set into a solid concrete or asphalt base, used for marking datums.
9. False Section 6 is always in the northwest or upper left-hand corner.
10. True

MULTIPLE CHOICE

1. B
2. B There are two parcels in this description denoted by the semicolon (:). The first: 1/4 of 640 = 160; 1/4 of 160 = 40. The second: 1/4 x 640 = 160 x 1/4 = 40 x ½ = 20. 20 + 40 = 60
3. B 43,560 x 6 = 261,360 square feet x $2.25 = $588,060
4. B A township is numbered in an"s" fashion: 1 through 6, right to left and 7 to 12, left to right. Section 7 is directly south of section 6.
5. D A benchmark is a permanent reference point used as a reference for marking datums.
6. C A metes-and-bounds description must always begin and end at the point of beginning; thus "encircling" the described property.
7. C A quarter of 640 acres is 160 acres.
8. A The U.S. Geological Survey datum is defined as the mean sea level at New York Harbor. A surveyor uses the datum to determine the height of a structure or to establish the grade of a street.
9. C 1/4 x 640 = 160 x 1/4 = 40 x 1/4 = 10 x $1,200 = $12,000
10. C
11. C
12. A
13. A
14. B
15. D 120 x 90 = 10,800 x 2 = 21,600

10

Real Estate Taxes and Other Liens

Matching (A)

Write the matching term on the appropriate line.

- ad valorem
- equitable lien
- subordination
- involuntary lien
- lien
- priority
- specific lien
- general lien
- taxes
- voluntary lien

1. ______________ A charge or claim against a person's property, to enforce the payment of money
2. ______________ A lien that is created intentionally by the property owner's action
3. ______________ A lien created by law
4. ______________ A lien that arises out of common law
5. ______________ A lien that affects all the real and personal property owned by a debtor
6. ______________ A lien that is secured by certain property
7. ______________ The order in which claims against property will be satisfied
8. ______________ A written agreement between lienholders to change the priority of a lien
9. ______________ Charges imposed by state and local governments to fund their functions and services
10. ______________ A general recurring real estate tax

True or False

Circle the answer

1. T F A voluntary lien may be classified as either statutory or equitable.
2. T F A charge or claim against a person's property by a creditor, made to enforce the payment of money, is referred to as a lien.
3. T F All encumbrances are liens.
4. T F Both federal estate taxes and state inheritance taxes are general, statutory and involuntary liens.
5. T F Taking out a mortgage loan is an example of the creation of an equitable lien.
6. T F A lien attaches to real property at the time the lien is filed.
7. T F A special assessment is always a specific, statutory and involuntary lien.
8. T F A court's decree that establishes the amount owed by a debtor is enforced by a judgment directing the sheriff to seize and sell the debtor's property.

Flash Cards (Pull out page & cut with scissors)

ad valorem tax	mortgage lien
judgment lien	redemption period
lien	satisfaction piece
lis pendens	special assessment
mechanic's lien	specific lien
mill	subordination

Lien on the property of a mortgagor (owner) that provides security for a loan

Chapter 10

Tax levied according to value, used to refer to real estate taxes

Chapter 10

Time frame in which property owners in some states have the right to redeem their real estate by paying the sales price, interest and costs

Chapter 10

After judgment entered and recorded with county recorder, becomes a general lien on defendant's real and personal property

Chapter 10

Document acknowledging that the debt has been repaid

Chapter 10

Right given by law to certain creditors to have their debts paid out of the property of a defaulting debtor, usually by court sale

Chapter 10

Tax or levy against only the properties that will benefit from a proposed public improvement like a sewer or paving a street

Chapter 10

Recorded legal document giving constructive notice that the property is the subject of an action filed in a state or federal court

Chapter 10

Lien affecting or attaching only to a certain, specific parcel of land

Chapter 10

Statutory lien in the property where contractors or materialmen have labor or materials in a given property

Chapter 10

Written agreement between lien holders that changes the priority of mortgage, judgment and other liens under certain circumstances

Chapter 10

One-tenth of one cent used in some states to compute real estate taxes; i.e., 52 mills = $0.052 tax for each dollar of assessed valuation of a property

Chapter 10

True or False (Continued)

9. T F Mechanics' liens never take priority over tax or special assessment liens.

10. T F "Ad valorem" taxes apply to the difference between the assessed value of a property and the value added by resale or improvement.

11. T F All liens are encumbrances.

12. T F The presence of a lien on real property does not prevent the owner from conveying title to another party.

13. T F A taxing body determines the appropriate tax rate by dividing the total monies needed for the coming fiscal year by the total assessments of all real estate located within the taxing body's jurisdiction.

14. T F A delinquent taxpayer may redeem property at any time prior to a tax sale by exercising his or her statutory right of redemption.

15. T F A mechanic's lien is a specific, involuntary lien.

Matching (B)

Write the matching term on the appropriate line.

- assessment
- money judgment
- equalization factor
- equitable right of redemption
- lis pendens
- attachment
- mechanic's lien
- mill
- special assessments
- statutory right of redemption

1. ______________ The official process of valuing real estate for tax purposes
2. ______________ A device to achieve uniformity in statewide assessments
3. ______________ 1/1,000 of a dollar, or $.001
4. ______________ The right of a delinquent taxpayer to recover property before a tax sale
5. ______________ The right of a delinquent taxpayer to recover property after a tax sale
6. ______________ Taxes levied on specific properties that benefit from public improvements
7. ______________ A specific, involuntary lien that gives security to persons or companies who perform labor or furnish material to improve real property
8. ______________ A court decree that establishes the amount owed by a debtor and provides for money to be awarded
9. ______________ A notice of a possible future lien based on a lawsuit
10. ______________ A writ that permits a court to retain custody of a debtor's property until the creditor's lawsuit is concluded

Lien Characteristics

Identify the characteristics of liens by placing check marks in the appropriate columns

Type of Lien	General	Specific	Voluntary	Involuntary	Equitable	Statutory
Mechanic's Lien						
Special Assessment						
Mortgage						
Bail Bond						
Utility Lien						
Federal Estate Lien						
Corporate Franchise Tax						
State Inheritance Tax						
Judgement						
Real Property Tax						

Multiple Choice

Circle A, B, C or D

1. Generally, in a court-ordered sale, which of the following is paid first?
   A. First mortgage
   B. Mechanic's liens
   C. Child support liens
   D. Real estate taxes

2. All of the following are examples of general liens. Which is an example of a specific lien?
   A. Decedent's debts
   B. Internal Revenue Service liens
   C. Mortgage lien
   D. Corporate franchise liens

3. The millage breakout for ad valorem taxes: library: .5; school: 1; school debt service: .5; community college: 1; vocational school: .5, and all others: 5. If the property is assessed at $165,000, how much is the tax bill?
   A. $1,200
   B. $1,402.50
   C. $1,405.75
   D. $1,800

4. All of the following are liens against real property EXCEPT
   A. a mortgage.
   B. real estate taxes.
   C. lis pendens.
   D. secured debts of a deceased property owner.

5. What is a real estate tax lien?
   A. Specific, involuntary lien
   B. Specific, voluntary lien
   C. General, involuntary lien
   D. General, voluntary lien

6. Which of the following may be either an involuntary or a voluntary lien on real property?
   A. Mortgage loan
   B. Real estate tax
   C. Special assessment
   D. Mechanic's lien

Multiple Choice (Continued)

7. Which of the following would permit a law enforcement officer to seize a debtor's property?
   A. lis pendens
   B. satisfaction of judgment
   C. writ of execution
   D. writ of attachment

8. If the property owners in a neighborhood petition the city for new sidewalks and paved alleys, which of the following best describes the character of the lien that may result if the city agrees to the improvements?
   A. general, statutory and voluntary
   B. specific, equitable and involuntary
   C. specific, statutory and voluntary
   D. general, equitable and involuntary

9. Which of the following is a general, statutory and involuntary lien on both real and personal property?
   A. federal tax lien
   B. mechanic's lien
   C. special assessment
   D. consumer loan lien

10. The owner stopped making mortgage payments to M in June. In February, the owner contracted with B to have his billiard room converted into a sauna and never paid for the work. The owner is two years delinquent in property taxes to county V and owes more than $30,000 on a custom luxury automobile purchased from D in January. The state gives mechanics' liens priority.

    If all these creditors obtain judgments against the owner in November, what will be the priority of their liens (first to last)?
    A. D –> B –> M –> V
    B. V –> M –> B –> D
    C. B –> V –> D –> M
    D. V –> B –> M –> D

11. A town wants to construct new concrete curbs in a residential neighborhood. How will the town most likely raise the money necessary for the improvement?
    A. ad valorem tax
    B. special assessment
    C. equalized assessment
    D. utility lien

12. All of the following liens must be recorded to be effective EXCEPT
    A. money judgment.
    B. mechanic's lien.
    C. real estate tax lien.
    D. voluntary lien.

13. The market value of an undeveloped parcel is $20,000. Its assessed value is 40 percent of market value, and properties in its county are subject to an equalization factor of 1.50. If the tax rate is $4 per $100, what is the amount of the tax owed on the property?
    A. $320
    B. $480
    C. $800
    D. $1,200

14. To establish a potential claim against the property and to establish priority, one needs to file a(n)
    A. lis pendens.
    B. attachment.
    C. general lien.
    D. specific lien.

15. G was considering having a new garage built. G talked about the project with several contractors, including Y. In April, while G was on vacation, Y began building the garage according to G's specifications. Work was completed by the end of May. In June, G returned from vacation and refused to pay for the garage. Y decides to file a mechanic's lien in July. Is Y entitled to a lien?
    A. Yes, because the garage was constructed according to G's specifications.
    B. Yes, because the garage is not a part of an owner-occupied residence.
    C. No, because notice of the lien should have been filed in May, when the work was completed.
    D. No, because there was no express or implied contract between G and Y.

Answer Key

MATCHING (A)

1. lien
2. voluntary lien
3. involuntary lien
4. equitable lien
5. general lien
6. specific lien
7. priority
8. subordination
9. taxes
10. ad valorem

TRUE OR FALSE

1. False An involuntary lien may be classified as either statutory or equitable.
2. True
3. False Not all encumbrances are liens.
4. True
5. False Taking out a mortgage loan is an example of the creation of a voluntary lien.
6. True
7. False A special assessment is always a specific and statutory lien, but may be either involuntary or voluntary, depending on the nature of the improvement being funded.
8. False A court's decree that establishes the amount owed by a debtor is enforced by a writ of execution directing the sheriff to seize and sell the debtor's property.
9. True
10. False "Ad valorem" taxes are based on the value of the property being taxed.
11. True
12. True
13. True
14. False A delinquent taxpayer may redeem property any time prior to a tax sale by exercising his or her equitable right of redemption.
15. True

MATCHING (B)

1. assessment
2. equalization factor
3. mill
4. equitable right of redemption
5. statutory right of redemption
6. special assessments
7. mechanic's lien
8. money judgment
9. lis pendens
10. attachment

MULTIPLE CHOICE ANSWERS

1. D Real estate taxes do not have to be recorded to be effective, and they take precedence over all other liens.
2. C A mortgage lien is a specific, voluntary lien.
3. B .5 + 1 + .5 + 1 +.5 + 5 = 8.5 mills or $.0085
   $165,000 x .0085 = $1,402.50
4. C A lis pendens is only the notice of a possible, future lien. However, if it becomes a lien, the priority is established by the date and time that the lis pendens was originally filed.
5. A A real estate tax is levied on an individual property; few would argue that individuals choose to have the tax levied, hence, an involuntary lien.
6. C If property owners request that the city or county make a repair and agree to a special assessment, it is considered voluntary. In other situations, the property owners may fight the proposed improvement, and the special assessment is therefore involuntary.
7. C A writ of execution directs the sheriff to seize and sell as much of the debtor's property as necessary to pay both the debt and the expenses of the sale.

Answer Key (Continued)

8. C Since the property owners have petitioned the city to make the improvements, the lien is voluntary. It will be levied on only the properties that receive the benefit, therefore it is specific. It is created by statute.

9. A An Internal Revenue Service lien is a general lien against the person; i.e., against the real and personal property owned by the delinquent taxpayer.

10. D The priority is taxes, mechanic's lien, first mortgage, and then personal property. Although the mortgage was filed first, property taxes always have first priority, and the state has given second priority to mechanic's liens. The personal property lien is last in priority.

11. B The town will levy a specific lien against the benefiting properties to pay for the new concrete curbs.

12. C Ad valorem real estate tax liens do not have to be recorded to be effective, and they always take precedence over all other liens. This is why most lenders collect 1/12 of the taxes each month, so that the lender can pay the taxes when due. Unpaid taxes would move ahead of the first mortgage.

13. B $20,000 x 40% x 1.5 ÷ 100 x 4 = $480

14. A A lis pendens is a notice of a possible future lien. If it becomes an actual lien, the effective date of the lien is the date and time that the lis pendens was filed.

15. D The contractor was in no way given authority to act; therefore, he or she has no right to file a mechanic's lien.

LIEN CHARACTERISTICS

Type of Lien	General	Specific	Voluntary	Involuntary	Equitable	Statutory
Mechanic's Lien		√		√	√	
Special Assessment		√	√	√		√
Mortgage		√	√		√	
Bail Bond		√	√			√
Utility Lien		√		√	√	
Federal Estate Lien	√			√		√
Corporate Franchise Tax	√			√		√
State Inheritance Tax	√			√		√
Judgement	√			√	√	
Real Property Tax		√		√		√

11

Real Estate Contracts

Matching (A)

Write the matching term on the appropriate line.

- bilateral contract
- consideration
- contract
- executed contract
- executory contract
- express contract
- implied contract
- mutual assent
- offeree
- unilateral contract

1. ______________ A voluntary, legally enforceable promise between legally competent parties
2. ______________ A contract in which the parties show their intention in words
3. ______________ A contract established by the acts and conduct of the parties
4. ______________ A contract in which both parties promise to perform some act
5. ______________ A one-sided agreement
6. ______________ A contract that has been completely performed
7. ______________ The status of a real estate sales contract prior to closing
8. ______________ The person who accepts the offer in a contract
9. ______________ Complete agreement about the purpose and terms of a contract
10. ______________ Something of legal value offered by one party and accepted by another as an inducement to act or refrain from acting

True or False

Circle the answer

1. T F An agreement to be bound by most of the terms proposed in an offer constitutes acceptance.
2. T F All contracts must be in writing to be enforceable.
3. T F A listing agreement is a contract for the sale of real estate.
4. T F Consideration is something of legal value offered by one party and accepted by the other as an inducement to act.
5. T F In an implied contract, the actual agreement between the parties is inferred from general or vague statements in the written agreement itself.

Flash Cards *(Pull out page & cut with scissors)*

assignment	liquidated damages
bilateral vs. unilateral contract	option
breach of contract	statute of frauds
consideration	time is of the essence
express vs. implied contract	unenforceable contract
installment contract	void vs. voidable

Amount predetermined by parties to contract as total compensation due injured party should the other party breach the contract

Chapter 11

Agreement to keep open for a set period an offer to sell or purchase property; usually a unilateral contract; one party must perform if the other so decides

Chapter 11

State law requires certain instruments, such as deeds, real estate sales contracts and certain leases, to be in writing to be legally enforceable

Chapter 11

Phrase in contract that requires the performance of a certain act within a stated period of time

Chapter 11

Contract that has all the elements of a valid contract, yet neither party can sue the other for performance; an unsigned contract is usually unenforceable

Chapter 11

Void has no legal force because it is lacking an essential part of a contract; void<u>able</u> is one in which either or both parties may reject or disaffirm (contingencies)

Chapter 11

Transfer in writing of interest in a bond, mortgage, lease

Chapter 11

Bilateral contract: both parties are legally bound to act as they promised, i.e. lease, purchase agreement unilateral contract: only one party is bound to act (option, promissory note)

Chapter 11

Failure to perform a condition of a contract, such as not paying the rent or a mortgage payment

Chapter 11

Something of value that gets a person to enter into a contract; owner of property promises to convey marketable title and the buyer promises a certain amount of money

Chapter 11

Express is oral or written contract in which parties express intentions in words. An implied contract is a result of the actions of the parties.

Chapter 11

Also known as land contract, contract for deed, selling under contract. Purchaser receives possession but not legal title until all payments have been made

Chapter 11

True or False (Continued)

6. T F The difference between a bilateral and a unilateral contract is the number of parties involved.

7. T F A sales contract is an executory contract from the time it is signed until closing; at closing, it becomes an executed contract.

8. T F A contract that may be rescinded or disaffirmed by one or both of the parties based on some legal principle is void, even though it may appear on the surface to be valid.

9. T F The person who makes an offer is the offeree; the person who accepts or rejects the offer is the offeror.

10. T F A contract entered into by a mentally ill person is voidable during the illness and for some time after the individual is cured.

11. T F An oral agreement for the sale of real estate is unenforceable.

12. T F Under a land contract, the buyer obtains both possession and title to the property by agreeing to make regular monthly payments to the seller over a number of years.

13. T F Assignment is the substitution of a new contract in place of the original one, while novation is a transfer of rights or duties under a contract.

14. T F An offer or counteroffer may be revoked at any time prior to its acceptance.

15. T F An option contract is an agreement by which the optionee gives the optionor the right to buy or lease property at a fixed price within a specific period of time.

16. T F Commingling occurs when a broker mixes his or her personal funds with a buyer's earnest money deposit.

17. T F The interest held by a buyer during the time between the signing of a sales contract and the transfer of title is known as equitable title.

18. T F An addendum is an additional, new provision that is added to an existing contract without altering the content of the original.

19. T F An option agreement is a unilateral contract.

20. T F A contract entered into by a minor is void.

Multiple Choice

Circle A, B, C or D

1. Which of the following is an example of a unilateral contract?
   A. Lease
   B. Agreement of sale
   C. Option
   D. Listing agreement

2. The seller accepted all of the terms that the buyer offered, making only one small change in the amount of the earnest money. At the moment, these agreements constitute a(n)
   A. offer.
   B. counter-offer.
   C. acceptance.
   D. rejection.

3. The buyer changed her mind about buying that particular lot. She called her agent and said, "Do not present my offer." Her action is called a(n)
   A. counter-offer.
   B. rejection.
   C. breach of contract.
   D. revocation.

4. A real estate broker announces to the salespeople in her office that she will pay a $1,000 bonus to the top-selling salesperson each quarter. This contract is a(n)
   A. implied bilateral contract.
   B. express unilateral contract.
   C. implied unilateral contract.
   D. express bilateral contract

Multiple Choice (Continued)

5. G makes an offer on a house, and R, the seller, accepts. What is the current status of this relationship?
   A. G and R do not have a valid contract until R delivers title at closing.
   B. G and R have an express, bilateral executed contract.
   C. G and R have an express, bilateral executory contract.
   D. G and R have an implied, unilateral executory contract.

6. F offers to buy M's house for the full $95,000 asking price. The offer contains the following clause: "Possession of the premises on August 1." M is delighted to accept F's offer, and signs the contract. First, however, M crosses out "August 1" and replaces it with "August 3," because M won't be back from vacation on the first of the month. M then begins scheduling movers. What is the status of this agreement?
   A. Because M's change was minor, F and M have a valid contract.
   B. M has accepted F's offer: the change is of no legal effect once the contract has been signed.
   C. M has rejected F's offer and made a counteroffer, which F is free to accept or reject.
   D. While M technically rejected F's offer, M's behavior in scheduling movers creates an implied contract between the parties.

7. A contract that is entered into by a person who is under the age of contractual capacity is
   A. unenforceable.
   B. void.
   C. voidable.
   D. valid

8. T is buying K's house and agrees to assume K's mortgage. The lender agrees and releases K from the obligation, substituting T as the party primarily liable for the debt. Which of the following terms best describes this transaction?
   A. assignment
   B. novation
   C. conversion
   D. consideration

9. Q and B enter into an oral agreement for the sale of a Farm. B changes his mind, and Q suffers a financial loss of $1,500. Which of the following best describes Q's position?
   A. Q may sue B for specific performance under the statute of frauds, forcing the sale of the farm.
   B. Q may sue B to recover the $1,500 loss, but may not compel B to perform.
   C. Q has no legal remedy, because this transaction should have been in writing as required by the statute of frauds.
   D. Q may sue for specific performance, but may not sue to recover monetary damages alone.

10. On March 7, N and L execute a contract for the purchase of N's property. Closing is set for June 10. On April 15, the property is struck by lightning and virtually destroyed by the resulting fire. If the Uniform Vendor and Purchaser Risk Act has been adopted by the state in which the property is located, which party bears liability for the loss?
    A. N and L share the loss equally under the Act.
    B. N bears the loss alone.
    C. L bears the loss alone, by virtue of her equitable title.
    D. Neither N nor L bears the loss.

11. R is trying to sell Dreadful Manor, but is having difficulty finding a buyer. H wants to buy Dreadful Manor but isn't sure whether or not she will be transferred out of the country by her employer. R agrees to accept a $500 payment from H, in return for which Dreadful Manor will be taken off the market for three months. H may purchase Dreadful Manor for a certain price any time during that period. This is a(n)
    A. unenforceable contract.
    B. land contract.
    C. sales contract.
    D. option contract.

12. All the following are essential to a valid real estate sales contract EXCEPT
    A. a written agreement, signed by both parties.
    B. consideration.
    C. an earnest money deposit, held in an escrow account.
    D. legally competent parties.

Multiple Choice (Continued)

13. A 14 year-old comes into a brokerage office and says, "I want to make an offer on the Walnut Street property. Here is a certified check for 10 percent of the asking price. Please help me with the paperwork." Why should the broker be concerned?
    A. A contract for the sale of real estate in which one of the parties is a minor is illegal.
    B. The earnest money deposit must be at least 20 percent of the asking price when a minor is involved in the transaction.
    C. The sales contract may be disaffirmed by the minor when he or she reaches the age of majority.
    D. The sales contract will be void because the minor's age is a matter of public record.

14. In case the buyer decides not to buy for no legal reason, the earnest money is there as
    A. actual damages.
    B. nominal damages.
    C. punitive damages.
    D. liquidated damages.

15. The buyer and seller agreed to a closing date of Sept 7, "time is of the essence." Which of the following is the closest meaning of the phrase?
    A. It would be very nice if both parties can have their affairs together to close on that date.
    B. If closing is not held on September 7, there is an automatic extension built in.
    C. Closing must be on or before September 7.
    D. If either party gives notice, the date can be moved back.

Matching (B)

Write the matching term on the appropriate line.

- void
- assignment
- breach
- contingencies
- earnest money
- land contract
- liquidated damages
- equitable title
- listing agreement
- novation

1. ________________ A contract that is without legal force or effect
2. ________________ The transfer of rights or duties under a contract
3. ________________ The substitution of a new contract to replace an earlier one
4. ________________ A violation of any of the terms or conditions of a contract without legal excuse
5. ________________ An employment contract between a broker and a seller
6. ________________ A deposit customarily made by a prospective purchaser when making an offer
7. ________________ The interest held by a buyer prior to delivery and acceptance of the deed
8. ________________ An amount of money that the parties agree will be the complete compensation available in the event of a breach
9. ________________ Additional conditions that must be satisfied before a sales contract is fully enforceable
10. ________________ A contract under which the seller retains title to property but the buyer obtains possession

Figure 11.1

Sample Residential Sales Contract

Agreement for Sale of Real Estate

BUYER(S): ______________________________

Address: ______________________________

City: ______________ State: ___ Zip ________ agrees to purchase, and

SELLER(S): ______________________________

Address: ______________________________

City: ______________ State: ___ Zip ________ agrees to sell to Buyer(s)

at the Price of : ______________________ Dollars ($__________)

the Property commonly described as ______________________________

(City of ______________, County of ______________ State of __________)

1. PROPERTY DESCRIPTION: "the Property," a complete legal description of which may be attached to this contract by either party. The Property has approximate lot dimensions of ______________, together with all existing improvements and fixtures, if any, to be transferred to the Buyer(s) by Bill of Sale at the time of closing, including (but not limited to): hot water heater, furnace, plumbing and electrical fixtures, sump pumps, central heating and cooling systems, fixed floor coverings, built-in kitchen appliances and cabinets, storm and screen windows and doors, window treatment hardware, shelving systems, all planted vegetation, garage door openers and car units, and the following items of personal property:

2. EARNEST MONEY: Buyer has paid $____________ by check by note (*delete one*), and will pay within _____ days the further sum of $______________, as earnest money to be applied against the purchase price. The earnest money shall be held by the Listing Broker for the mutual benefit of the parties. The balance of the purchase price, $______________, shall be paid in full at closing.

3. CLOSING DATE: The closing date shall be ______________, 19__, at ______________.

4. POSSESSION: Possession shall be at closing.

5. COMMISSION: Seller(s) agree that ______________, Listing Broker, brought about this sale and agrees to pay a Broker's commission as agreed in the listing agreement.

6. FINANCING: This contract is subject to the condition that Buyer(s) shall, by ____________, 19 __, obtain a written commitment for a loan secured by a mortgage or deed of trust on the Property in the amount of $______________. Financing shall be secured in the form of a mortgage of the following type:(delete those items that do not apply) Conventional (fixed or adjustable rate); FHA mortgage; VA mortgage; assumption of existing mortgage; financing by Seller(s).

Sales Contract

Figure 11.1 on the preceding page is the first page of a standard real estate sales contract. Fill it in using information from the narrative below:

You are the buyer. The date is today. The property is 1105 Azalea Street in Poleduck County, city of Pleasant Valley, Virginia 98765. The lot dimensions are 70 by 160 feet. The sellers are Paul and Polly Purveyor, who currently live in the house being sold.

The buyer is particularly insistent that the kitchen appliances (a stove, dishwasher and refrigerator) convey with the property, and that an outdoor gas cooker and swingset stay as well. The earnest money deposit is 15 percent of the purchase price of $117,500, paid by check, with an additional 10 percent of the balance due in one business week.

The closing will take place exactly 64 days from today at the office of the buyer's attorney, R. Tassel. The financing will be by conventional, fixed-rate mortgage, in the amount of the balance due. The buyer will not accept an interest rate greater than 7.5 percent. The commitment date is two weeks from today. The listing broker is F. J. Broker.

Answer Key

MATCHING (A)

1. contract
2. express contract
3. implied contract
4. bilateral contract
5. unilateral contract
6. executed contract
7. executory contract
8. offeree
9. mutual assent
10. consideration

TRUE OR FALSE

1. False An agreement to be bound by all of the terms proposed in an offer constitutes acceptance.
2. False While a contract may be written or oral, certain types of contracts must be in writing to be enforceable.
3. False A listing agreement is an employment contract between a broker and a seller.
4. True
5. False In an implied contract, the actual agreement between the parties is demonstrated by their acts and conduct.
6. False The difference between a bilateral and a unilateral contract is the presence or absence of the exchange of mutual promises.
7. True
8. False A contract that may be rescinded or disaffirmed by one or both of the parties based on some legal principle is voidable, even though it may appear on the surface to be valid
9. False The person who makes an offer is the offeror; the person who accepts or rejects the offer is the offeree.
10. True
11. True
12. False Under a land contract, the buyer obtains possession but not title to the property by agreeing to make regular monthly payments to the seller over a number of years.
13. False Novation is the substitution of a new contract in place of the original one, while assignment is a transfer of rights or duties under a contract
14. True

Answer Key (Continued)

15. False An option contract is an agreement by which the optionor gives the optionee the right to buy or lease property at a fixed price within a specific period of time.
16. True
17. True
18. True
19. True
20. False A contract entered into by a minor is voidable.

MULTIPLE CHOICE ANSWERS

1. C The optionor/owner of the property must sell at the agreed upon price only IF the optionee decides to buy. Only one party is obligated to perform.
2. B Even changing one "small" term constitutes a rejection and a new counter-offer which the other party is not under obligation to accept.
3. D The buyer may revoke her offer anytime until she is notified that the seller has accepted the offer.
4. B This is an express contract since the broker clearly stated her intentions to the salespeople. It is an unilateral contract since she is obligated to keep her promise, but the salespeople are not obligated to perform.
5. C The seller has promised to sell; the buyer has promised to buy; clearly a bilateral contract and express, since they announced their intentions in writing.
6. C Even changing the smallest of terms, for whatever reason, constitutes a rejection and counter-offer, which the other party is not under obligation to accept.
7. C The underage party may void the contract, but the older party who entered into the contract with the minor is obligated to perform.
8. B Substituting a new obligation or new parties to an old, existing contract is known as novation. In this situation, it is also called "release of liability."
9. B Verbal agreements to buy and sell real estate are unenforceable in a court of law. Q can sue B for the loss.
10. B In states that have adopted the Uniform Vendor and Purchaser Act, the seller remains responsible for the property until the day of closing.
11. D H has the right to buy at an agreed upon price within a certain time frame, but she doesn't have to. R will have to sell to H within that time frame whether or not he receives a higher offer from another prospect.
12. C Earnest money is an option to a contract, not a requirement. It is available for liquidated damages. The consideration is the exchange of promises, i.e., the seller promises marketable title and the buyer promises a certain amount of money.
13. C A minor may void the contract citing "I am underage." A minor's guardian may purchase for the minor.
14. D Liquidated damages limits the compensation available to the injured party should a breach of contract occur.
15. C Time is of the essence requires that the contract be completed during that time frame or the party who fails to perform on time is liable for breach of contract.

MATCHING (B)

1. void
2. assignment
3. novation
4. breach
5. listing agreement
6. earnest money
7. equitable title
8. liquidated damages
9. contingencies
10. land contract

Answer Key (Continued)

Agreement for Sale of Real Estate

BUYER(S): Student's Name

Address: Student's Address

City: ______ State: ___ Zip ______ agrees to purchase, and

SELLER(S): Paul and Polly Purveyor (h/w)

Address: 1105 Azalea St.

City: Pleasant Valley State: VA Zip 98765 agrees to sell to Buyer(s)

at the Price of : One Hundred Seventeen Thousand Five Hundred Dollars ($117,500)

the Property commonly described as 1105 Azalea St.

(City of Pleasant Valley, County of Poleduck State of Virginia)

1. PROPERTY DESCRIPTION: "the Property," a complete legal description of which may be attached to this contract by either party. The Property has approximate lot dimensions of 70' by 160', together with all existing improvements and fixtures, if any, to be transferred to the Buyer(s) by Bill of Sale at the time of closing, including (but not limited to): hot water heater, furnace, plumbing and electrical fixtures, sump pumps, central heating and cooling systems, fixed floor coverings, built-in kitchen appliances and cabinets, storm and screen windows and doors, window treatment hardware, shelving systems, all planted vegetation, garage door openers and car units, and the following items of personal property:

   Kitchen stove, dishwasher, refrigerator, outdoor gas cooker and swing set

2. EARNEST MONEY: Buyer has paid $17,625.00 by check ~~by note~~ (*delete one*), and will pay within 5 days the further sum of $9,987.50, as earnest money to be applied against the purchase price. The earnest money shall be held by the Listing Broker for the mutual benefit of the parties. The balance of the purchase price, $89,887.50, shall be paid in full at closing.

3. CLOSING DATE: The closing date shall be today + 64 days, 19__, at Law Office of R. Tassel.

4. POSSESSION: Possession shall be at closing.

5. COMMISSION: Seller(s) agree that F. J. Broker, Listing Broker, brought about this sale and agrees to pay a Broker's commission as agreed in the listing agreement.

6. FINANCING: This contract is subject to the condition that Buyer(s) shall, by today + 2 wks, 19 __, obtain a written commitment for a loan secured by a mortgage or deed of trust on the Property in the amount of $89, 887.50. Financing shall be secured in the form of a mortgage of the following type:(delete those items that do not apply) Conventional (fixed ~~or adjustable~~ rate); ~~FHA mortgage; VA mortgage; assumption of existing mortgage; financing by Seller(s)~~. Not to exceed 7.5 %

12 Transfer of Title

Matching (A)

Write the matching term on the appropriate line.

- acknowledgment
- deed
- deed in trust
- grantee
- quiet enjoyment
- grantor
- granting clause
- seisin
- title
- voluntary alienation

1. ____________ The right to and evidence of ownership of land
2. ____________ The transfer of title by gift or sale
3. ____________ A written instrument by which an owner conveys the right, title or interest in a parcel of real estate to someone else
4. ____________ The person who transfers title
5. ____________ The person who acquires title by gift or sale
6. ____________ A statement of the intention to convey property by deed
7. ____________ A formal declaration, made before a notary public, that the person who is signing the deed is doing so voluntarily and that his or her signature is genuine
8. ____________ A covenant that the grantor is the owner of the property and has the right to convey it
9. ____________ A guarantee that the grantee's title will be good against any third party who might bring legal action to establish superior title
10. ____________ A conveyance by deed from a trustor to a trustee

True or False

Circle the answer

1. T F A title to real estate is a printed document signed by the secretary of state.
2. T F A deed is the written instrument by which an owner of real estate intentionally conveys the right, title or interest in a parcel to someone else.
3. T F To be valid, a deed must include a recital of consideration, an identifiable grantee and a recital of exceptions and reservations.
4. T F A title is considered transferred when the deed is actually signed and acknowledged by the grantor.
5. T F To be valid, a deed must be signed by both the grantor and the grantee.
6. T F In a special warranty deed, the covenant of seisin warrants that the grantor's title will be good against third parties.

Flash Cards *(Pull out page & cut with scissors)*

acknowledgment	**intestate**
adverse possession	**probate**
deed	**quiet enjoyment covenant**
general warranty deed	**quitclaim deed**
grantor, grantee	**transfer tax**
habendum clause	**will**

Person dies without a valid will; his or her property will pass to heirs as provided in the state law of descent

Chapter 12

Formal declaration by someone like a notary public, that the signature is both voluntary (no force) and genuine (no forgery)

Chapter 12

Legal process by which a court determines who will inherit a deceased person's property and what the assets of the estate are

Chapter 12

Possession of another's land as if the owner for a statutory period which may lead to acquiring title

Chapter 12

Clause in deed guaranteeing that the grantee's title will be good against third parties who might bring court action

Chapter 12

Written document that, when executed and delivered, conveys title to or an interest in real estate

Chapter 12

Offers the least protection of any deed; conveys a real estate interest, if any; often used to correct misspelled names, etc.

Chapter 12

Deed that offers the most protection in which grantor fully warrants good clear title to the premises

Chapter 12

Tax on the transfer of real property; may require that stamps be attached to deed

Chapter 12

In a deed, the grantor is the person transferring title in real estate to the grantee

Chapter 12

Written document, properly witnessed, providing for transfer of title to property owned by the deceased, called the testator

Chapter 12

"To have and to hold" clause in a deed defining the extent of ownership being granted; i.e., a life estate or a defeasible fee

Chapter 12

True or False (Continued)

7. T F In a general warranty deed, the covenant of further assurance represents a promise by the grantor that he or she will obtain and deliver any instrument needed to ensure good title.

8. T F A bargain and sale deed does not contain any express warranties against encumbrances.

9. T F If a trustee wanted to convey real estate back to the grantor, he or she would use a trustee's deed.

10. T F In a deed executed pursuant to court order, the full amount of consideration is stated in the deed.

11. T F Adverse possession is an example of involuntary alienation of property.

12. T F When a property owner dies, his or her heirs by descent or will may immediately take possession of any real estate.

13. T F While a deed must be delivered during the grantor's lifetime, a will takes effect only after the owner's death.

14. T F A person who receives real property through a testamentary transfer is referred to as the devisee.

15. T F Real property of an owner who dies intestate is distributed according to the laws of the state in which the owner resided at the time of his or her death.

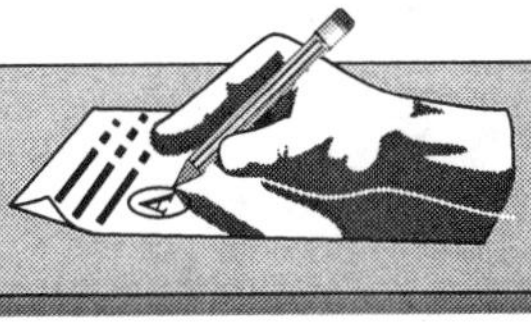

Multiple Choice

Circle A, B, C or D

1. The grantor is conveying an interest that is less than fee simple absolute. This explanation of the extent of ownership will be found in the
   A. seisen clause.
   B. granting clause.
   C. habendum clause.
   D. exceptions and reservations.

2. F conveys Happy Acres to R by a written document that contains five covenants protecting R's title. What is F's role in this transaction?
   A. Grantee
   B. Grantor
   C. Devisor
   D. Devisee

3. The verification that the grantor's signature is both genuine and voluntary is a(n)
   A. judgment.
   B. attachment.
   C. consideration.
   D. acknowledgment.

4. Here are some examples of voluntary alienation. Which is an example of involuntary alienation?
   A. Sale
   B. Gift
   C. Escheat
   D. Will

5. Who must sign the deed?
   A. Grantee only
   B. Grantor only
   C. Both grantor and grantee
   D. Grantor, grantee and registrar of deeds

6. The transfer of any interest in a parcel of real estate is typically in a document called the
   A. title.
   B. deed.
   C. attachment.
   D. mortgage.

7. All of the following are necessary to a valid deed EXCEPT
   A. recital of consideration.
   B. words of conveyance.
   C. grantee's signature.
   D. delivery.

Multiple Choice (Continued)

8. "I do hereby convey to my nearest relative all my interest in the property known as 123 Main Street, Elkhorn, West Dakota, to have and to hold, in consideration of receipt of the amount of $10 and other good and valuable consideration." When signed, this document is a(n)
   A. valid conveyance by deed.
   B. invalid conveyance by deed, because the property conveyed is inadequately described.
   C. invalid conveyance by deed, because there is no recital of exceptions and reservations.
   D. invalid conveyance by deed, because the grantee is inadequately identified.

9. The type of deed that imposes the least liability on a grantor is a
   A. special warranty deed.
   B. bargain and sale deed.
   C. quitclaim deed.
   D. general warranty deed.

10. Title is not considered transferred until the deed is
    A. signed by the grantor.
    B. delivered to and accepted by the grantee.
    C. delivered to the grantee.
    D. released from escrow.

11. Which of the following is a guarantee that the grantor has the right to convey the property?
    A. Covenant against encumbrances
    B. Covenant of seisin
    C. Covenant of further assurance
    D. Covenant of quiet enjoyment

12. A bargain and sale deed contains how many express warranties?
    A. 0
    B. 2
    C. 3
    D. 5

13. Which type of deed is used by a grantor whose interest in the real estate may be unknown?
    A. Bargain-and-sale deed
    B. Special warranty deed
    C. General warranty deed
    D. Quitclaim deed

14. Under the law of the state of North Michigan, 1/2 of an intestate decedent's property goes to his or her spouse, 1/4 of the remainder is divided equally among his or her children, and 1/4 goes to the state. If there is no spouse, the children divide 3/4 equally. K, a citizen of North Michigan, dies intestate, survived by an ex-spouse and seven adult children. If K's estate is $865,550, how much will each child receive under North Michigan law?
    A. $0
    B. $92,737.50
    C. $61,825
    D. $123,650

15. In East Carolina, the transfer tax is $1.20 for each $300 (or fraction of $300) of the sales price of any parcel of real estate. If a seller's property sold for $250,000, what will be the amount of the transfer tax due?
    A. $97
    B. $999.99
    C. $1,000.80
    D. $1,250.50

16. In front of witnesses, G says to R, "I never made a will, but I want you to have The Quarteracre Farm when I die." If R becomes the owner of The Quarteracre Farm, it is because the state recognizes what kind of will?
    A. Holographic
    B. Testamentary
    C. Nuncupative
    D. Probated

17. T inherited Stately Manor from his uncle in 1975. T has never visited Stately Manor or taken any responsibility for it. In 1978, without T's knowledge, L moved into the empty house. Between 1978 and 1992, L repaired and maintained Stately Manor as if it were her own home. She invited neighbors to attend holiday parties on the grounds. In 1992, L moved out of Stately Manor, and her son moved in. If the applicable period for adverse possession is 15 years, when can L's son claim title?
    A. L's son can claim title by adverse possession in the year 2007.
    B. L's son cannot claim title, because L failed to satisfy the requirements for adverse possession.
    C. L's son can claim title on the 15th anniversary of the date when L moved into Stately Manor.
    D. L's son cannot claim title, because T is the true legal owner of Stately Manor.

Multiple Choice (Continued)

18. In one state, the transfer tax is $0.80 per $500 or fraction thereof. There is no tax charged on the first $500 of the price. What tax must the seller pay if the property sells for $129,650?
    A. $205
    B. $206.64
    C. $206.40
    D. $207.44

19. A modification to the original will is called a(n)
    A. addendum.
    B. amendment.
    C. probate
    D. codicil.

20. All of the following are reasons for probate EXCEPT
    A. ensure that the heirs do not fight among themselves.
    B. confirm that the will is valid.
    C. determine the exact assets of the deceased person.
    D. identify which persons get any of the estate.

Deed Characteristics

Identify the characteristics of deeds by placing check marks in the appropriate columns

Figure 12.1

CHARACTERISTICS	TYPES OF DEEDS			
	General Warranty	Special Warranty	Bargain and Sale	Quitclaim
Covenant of Warranty Forever				
Covenant of Further Assurance				
Covenant of Quiet Enjoyment				
Covenant Against Encumberances				
Covenant of Seisin				
Express Warranties				
Implied Warranties				
Delivery and Acceptance				
Legal Description				
Habendum Clause				
Granting Clause				
Identifiable Grantee				
Signature of Grantor				
Consideration				
Grantor of Sound Mind				
Grantor of Lawful Age				

Matching (B)

Write the matching term on the appropriate line.

- reconveyance deed
- devise
- involuntary alienation
- probate
- quitclaim
- special warranty
- bargain and sale
- testate
- testator
- trustee's deed

1. ______________ A type of deed that warrants only that the grantor received title, and that the property has not been encumbered during the grantor's ownership
2. ______________ A deed that contains no express warranties, but that implies that the grantor holds title and possession of the property
3. ______________ A deed that contains no covenants, warranties or implications and that provides the least protection of any deed
4. ______________ A conveyance by deed from a trustee to anyone other than the trustor
5. ______________ A conveyance by deed from a trustee to the trustor
6. ______________ The transfer of title without the owner's consent
7. ______________ Having prepared a will indicating how property is to be disposed of after death
8. ______________ The gift of real property by will
9. ______________ The person who makes a will
10. ______________ A formal judiciary process to confirm a will's validity

Answer Key

MATCHING (A)

1. title
2. voluntary alienation
3. deed
4. grantor
5. grantee
6. granting clause
7. acknowledgment
8. seisin
9. quiet enjoyment
10. deed in trust

MATCHING (B)

1. special warranty
2. bargain and sale
3. quitclaim
4. trustee's deed
5. reconveyance deed
6. involuntary alienation
7. testate
8. devise
9. testator
10. probate

Answer Key (Continued)

TRUE OR FALSE

1. False A title to real estate is not an actual printed document.
2. True
3. False To be valid, a deed must include a recital of consideration and an identifiable grantee; a deed may contain a recital of exceptions and reservations.
4. False A title is considered transferred when the deed is actually delivered to the grantee by the grantor.
5. False To be valid, a deed must be signed by all grantors named in the deed.
6. False In a general warranty deed, the covenant of seisin warrants that the grantor is the owner of the property and has the right to convey it.
7. True
8. True
9. False If a trustee wanted to convey real estate back to the grantor, he or she would use a reconveyance deed.
10. True
11. True
12. False When a property owner dies, his or her heirs by descent or will immediately take title to the property, but may take possession only after probate.
13. True
14. True
15. False Real property of an owner who dies intestate is distributed according to the laws of the state in which the property is located.

MULTIPLE CHOICE ANSWERS

1. C The habendum clause is the "to have and to hold" clause which defines the extent of ownership that is being conveyed.
2. B Since F is conveying his or her interest, F is the grantor. The person who receives the interest is the grantee.
3. D The person who observes the signing and verifies its authenticity will often ask for a picture ID.
4. C Dying may not be voluntary, but writing a will is. When a person dies intestate and leaves no heirs, his or her estate will "escheat" back to the state.
5. B Because the grantor is giving up rights forever, the grantor must sign away those rights. The grantee receives the property; there is no need for the grantee's signature.
6. B A deed is the written document which transfers a real estate interest. Evidence of ownership (title) is written in the deed. An attachment is the process of taking a person's property into legal custody by a court order. A mortgage provides the security for a loan.
7. C See # 5. The grantee does not need to sign the deed since the grantee receives the property.
8. D Although the property may be adequately describe, the grantee is not sufficiently identified. There is no transfer.
9. C A quitclaim deed offers little or no protection. It transfers an interest, if any.
10. B The most complete answer is "delivered to and accepted by" the grantee during the grantor's lifetime.
11. B The covenant against encumbrances is a warranty that the property is free from encumbrances, except as so noted. The grantor further assures that he or she will do the needful to make the title good. Quiet enjoyment guarantees that the title will be good against third parties who might try to bring legal action to gain the property.
12. A A bargain and sale deed contains no express warranties against encumbrances, but it does imply that the grantor holds title and possession of the property.

Multiple Choice (Continued)

13. D A quitclaim deed is used to clear up clouds on the title. The grantor "quits" his or her claim, if any.

14. B The ex-spouse gets nothing. The state gets 1/4; and 3/4 will be divided equally among the seven children. \$865,550 ÷ 4 = \$216,387.50 to the state. The remaining amount (\$649,162.50) is divided seven ways leaving \$92,737.50 per child.

15. C \$250,000 ÷ 300 = 833.3333 or 834 x \$1.20 = \$1,000.80

16. C A holographic will is completely handwritten. A testamentary trust is established by will after the owner's death. Probate is the process of determining the validity of the will and distributing the assets of the estate.

17. C Although the son has not occupied the property very long, he can "tack" his adverse possession to that of his mother's. His mother's occupancy was certainly "open and notorious."

18. C \$129,650 minus the free \$500 ÷ \$500 increments = 258.3 rounded up to 258 x \$.80 = \$206.40

19. D Additional agreements attached to an agreement of sale are addenda; an amendment is a change to the existing content of a contract. Probate is the process of determining the validity of a will.

20. A Hopefully, the probate process will not anger too many heirs, but keeping them happy is not the reason for probate.

FIGURE 12.1

	TYPES OF DEEDS			
CHARACTERISTICS	**General Warranty**	**Special Warranty**	**Bargain and Sale**	**Quitclaim**
Covenant of Warranty Forever	√			
Covenant of Further Assurance	√			
Covenant of Quiet Enjoyment	√			
Covenant Against Encumbrances	√	√		
Covenant of Seisin	√	√		
Express Warranties	√	√		
Implied Warranties	√	√	√	
Delivery and Acceptance	√	√	√	√
Legal Description	√	√	√	√
Habendum Clause	√	√	√	√
Granting Clause	√	√	√	√
Identifiable Grantee	√	√	√	√
Signature of Grantor	√	√	√	√
Consideration	√	√	√	√
Grantor of Sound Mind	√	√	√	√
Grantor of Lawful Age	√	√	√	√

*NOTE ; The check marks in the top two boxes of the **Special Warranty Deed** column show that its basic warranties are similar to the **General Warranty**'s covenants of seisin and against encumbrances. Remember that a **Special Warranty Deed contains two warranties**: (1) that the grantor received title and (2) that the property was not encumbered during the time the grantor held it.*

Title Records

13

Matching

Write the matching term on the appropriate line.

- abstractor
- actual notice
- chain of title
- constructive notice
- title insurance
- recording
- security agreement
- priority
- suit to quiet title
- title search

1. ________________ The act of placing documents in the public record
2. ________________ The legal presumption that information may be obtained through diligent inquiry
3. ________________ A type of notice also known as "direct knowledge"
4. ________________ The order of rights in time
5. ________________ The record of a property's ownership
6. ________________ A legal action to remove a cloud on the title and establish legal ownership
7. ________________ An examination of all the public records to determine if any defects exist in a property's history of ownership
8. ________________ The individual who prepares a summary report of the results of a title search
9. ________________ A contract under which a policyholder is protected from losses arising from defects in title
10. ________________ A document required by the UCC for a lender to create a lienable interest in personal property

Circle the answer

True or False

1. T F Any individual who is interested in a particular property may review the public records to learn about the documents, claims and other issues that affect its ownership.
2. T F Any written document that affects any estate, right, title or interest in land must be recorded in the county in which the property owner resides.
3. T F To be eligible for recording, a document pertaining to real estate must be drawn and executed in accordance with the requirements of the UCC.
4. T F Constructive notice means that information about a property is not only available, but that someone has been given access to that information.
5. T F A search of the public records will disclose all liens that exist against a property.

True or False (Continued)

6. T F The term "chain of title" refers to the record of a property's ownership.

7. T F In a typical title search, the chain of title is examined, beginning with the earliest records of ownership and proceeding forward up to the present owner.

8. T F A standard coverage title insurance policy protects a homeowner against rights of parties in possession and unrecorded liens.

9. T F One of the requirements of marketable title is that it could convince a reasonably well-informed and prudent purchaser, acting on business principles and with full knowledge of the significant facts, that the property could be resold or mortgaged at a later time.

10. T F A certificate of title is a guarantee of legal ownership.

Multiple Choice

1. All of the following are acceptable evidence of an owner's title, EXCEPT a(n)
   A. abstract of title and attorney's opinion.
   B. recorded deed.
   C. title insurance policy.
   D. certificate of title.

2. Where is the deed recorded?
   A. City where owner lives
   B. County where property is located
   C. State capital
   D. Largest city in the state

3. P sells Newacre to Q. Five years ago, a lien was recorded against Newacre by Rabbit Construction Company. Newacre is in County 12, but the lien was recorded in County 21. When the lien was recorded, Q was an active partner in Rabbit Construction. A title search in County 12 disclosed no liens against Newacre. Which of the following is true?
   A. Q has constructive notice of the lien but not actual notice, because of the mistake in recording.
   B. Q has actual notice of the lien but not constructive notice, because of the mistake in recording.
   C. Q has both actual and constructive notice of the lien, because of his association with Rabbit Construction and the recorded lien.
   D. Q has no notice of the lien.

4. N purchased Blue Acres from M. Shortly after closing, N discovered that there were serious flaws in the title that made it unlikely that Blue Acres could be resold in the future. What can N do now?
   A. Because the title was flawed, N can legally void the sale, and M must return any consideration.
   B. N has no recourse.
   C. Because M conveyed unmarketable title, N is entitled to a new title report.
   D. Because N has accepted the deed, N's only recourse is to sue M under any covenants contained in the deed.

5. The reason that deeds and liens and other claims are recorded is to give
   A. constructive notice.
   B. actual notice.
   C. direct notice.
   D. nominal notice.

6. A history of all recorded liens and encumbrances is revealed in the
   A. title insurance policy.
   B. unrecorded documents.
   C. chain of title.
   D. abstract.

Flash Cards (Pull out page & cut with scissors)

abstract of title	priority
attorney's opinion of title	recording
certificate of title	subrogation
chain of title	suit to quiet title
constructive notice	title insurance
marketable title	Uniform Commercial Code

Order of position or time; priority of liens is by chronological order, first recorded having first claim except that taxes always have first place even if not recorded

Chapter 13

Certification by abstractor that condensed history of title to a particular parcel of real estate, including conveyances and encumbrances, is correct

Chapter 13

Act of entering documents affecting ownership or interests in real estate in the recorder's office established in each county

Chapter 13

Statement that attorney has certified an abstract to be an accurate statement of the facts concerning the property ownership

Chapter 13

Substitution of one creditor for another; used by title insurers to acquire from the injured party rights to sue in order to recover any claims they have paid

Chapter 13

Based on examination of public records, a statement of opinion on the status of the title to a parcel of real estate

Chapter 13

Court action intended to establish or settle the title to a particular property, especially when there is a cloud on the title

Chapter 13

Succession of conveyances from some accepted starting point, whereby the present holder of title derives the title; there should be no "breaks" in the succession

Chapter 13

Policy insuring the owner or mortgagee against loss by reason of defects in the title of a parcel of real estate

Chapter 13

Notice given to the world by recorded documents; possession of the property may also be considered constructive notice

Chapter 13

Concerned with personal property transactions, not real estate, governs the documents when personal property is used as security for a loan

Chapter 13

Good or clear title, reasonably free from the risk of litigation over possible defects

Chapter 13

Multiple Choice (Continued)

7. The person who prepares a certificate of title would be liable for which of the following?
   A. Parties in possession
   B. Negligence in preparing the certificate
   C. Fraudulent past conveyances
   D. Recorded transfers involved forged documents

8. Which of the following would be covered in a standard title insurance policy?
   A. Defects discoverable by physical inspection
   B. Unrecorded liens
   C. Forged documents
   D. Easements and restrictive covenants

9. A title insurance policy that protects the interests of a mortgagee is referred to as a(n)
   A. leasehold policy.
   B. lender's policy.
   C. certificate of sale policy.
   D. ALTA policy.

10. The Uniform Commercial Code applies to
   A. all real property transactions.
   B. sales and leases of commercial property.
   C. real property transactions involving a mortgage loan.
   D. personal property or fixtures used as security for a loan.

Figure 13.1

Tracing the Chain of Title

The abstract below illutrates the complete title record for Lot 27, Block 6 of Springfield Pines Subdivision. Indicate the point at which the chain of title is broken.

GRANTOR	GRANTEE	BY INSTRUMENT	CONVEYANCE DATE
Ferris - Bumper Builders, Inc.	Barton Doyle and Jane Doyle	Warranty Deed	January 19, 1909
Barton Doyle and Jane Doyle	Market Title & Trust Co.	Trust Deed	January 20, 1909
Market Title & Trust Co.	Barton Doyle and Jane Doyle	Reconveyance Deed	June 10, 1935
Barton Doyle and Jane Doyle	Anton Feldspar	Bargain and Sale Deed	March 7, 1940
Peter Parker and Mary Parker	Lamont Cranston and Gloria Reve	Warranty Deed	November 16, 1958
Lamont Cranston and Gloria Reve	Brookfield Bank and Trust Co.	Mortgage	November 8, 1958
Lamont Cranston and Gloria Reve	Gerald Carlos and Lydi Carlos	Warranty Deed	September 4, 1979
Brookfield Bank and Trust Co.	Lamont Cranston and Gloria Reve	Release	May 2, 1995

Answer Key

MATCHING

1. recording
2. constructive notice
3. actual notice
4. priority
5. chain of title
6. suit to quiet title
7. title search
8. abstractor
9. title insurance
10. security agreement

TRUE OR FALSE

1. True
2. False In most states, any written document that affects any estate, right, title or interest in land must be recorded in the county in which the property is located.
3. False To be eligible for recording, a document pertaining to real estate must be drawn and executed in accordance with the requirements of the recording acts of the state in which the property is located.
4. False Actual notice means that not only is the information about property available, but someone has been given access to that information.
5. False A search of the public records will disclose all recorded liens that exist against a property.
6. True
7. False In a typical title search, the chain of title is examined beginning with the present owner and tracing backwards to the earliest records of ownership.
8. False An extended coverage title insurance policy would protect a homeowner against rights of parties in possession and unrecorded liens.
9. True
10. False A certificate of title is evidence of ownership, but not a guarantee.

MULTIPLE CHOICE ANSWERS

1. B A recorded deed is nothing more than just that. A, C, and D are all verifications of thorough examinations of recorded documents that could affect the title.
2. B Since land is immobile, it makes sense to record all information about title to the property in the county where it is located. Owners move around all the time and would be hard to find.
3. B Because Q was a partner, he knew that the lien was filed. Constructive notice is not given because the lien was not filed in the county where the property is located, the place where it would be expected to be.
4. D This is an example why professionals should look at the evidence of ownership before closing. There is more leverage to get problems corrected before closing than after closing.
5. A The recorder's office is a central place to deposit and discover information. If it is recorded, then no one can say that he or she did not know. They would have known if they had researched the records.
6. D The title insurance policy lists coverage and exceptions to the policy. Unrecorded documents have not been examined. The chain of title traces ownership. The abstract is the most complete documentation of recorded liens and encumbrances.
7. B It is expected that the buyer will visit the property to determine if there is someone there who claims it. The person who does the search should be expected to find all recorded conveyances but is not expected to determine forgeries and authenticity of documents.

Answer Key (Multiple Choice - Continued)

8. C Title insurance does not protect against claims of parties in possession because the grantee should have visited the property, nor does it cover unrecorded liens. Easements and restrictive covenants are found in the deed and should be known to the grantee.

9. B The mortgagee is the lender. The mortgagee's policy is transferable.

10. D The Uniform Commercial Code does not apply to real estate. The UCC governs the documents when personal property is used as security for a loan.

TRACING THE CHAIN OF TITLE

GRANTOR	GRANTEE	BY INSTRUMENT	CONVEYANCE DATE
Ferris - Bumper Builders, Inc.	Barton Doyle and Jane Doyle	Warranty Deed	January 19, 1909
Barton Doyle and Jane Doyle	Market Title & Trust Co.	Trust Deed	January 20, 1909
Market Title & Trust Co.	Barton Doyle and Jane Doyle	Reconveyance Deed	June 10, 1935
Barton Doyle and Jane Doyle	Anton Feldspar	Bargain and Sale Deed	March 7, 1940
Peter Parker and Mary Parker	Lamont Cranston and Gloria Reve	Warranty Deed	November 16, 1958
Lamont Cranston and Gloria Reve	Brookfield Bank and Trust Co.	Mortgage	November 8, 1958
Lamont Cranston and Gloria Reve	Gerald Carlos and Lydi Carlos	Warranty Deed	September 4, 1979
Brookfield Bank and Trust Co.	Lamont Cranston and Gloria Reve	Release	May 2, 1995

In November of 1958, Peter and Mary Parker conveyed title as grantors, but there is no indication that they ever received title as grantees from Anton Feldspar.

14 Real Estate Financing: Principles

Matching (A)

Write the matching term on the appropriate line.

- acceleration clause
- hypothecation
- discount points
- execute
- deed of trust
- mortgagor
- mortgagee
- usury
- interest
- promissory note

1. ______________ The borrower in a mortgage loan
2. ______________ The lender in a mortgage loan
3. ______________ The act of signing a loan instrument
4. ______________ A borrower's personal pledge to repay a debt according to agreed-on terms
5. ______________ The pledging of a property as security for payment of a loan without actually surrendering the property itself
6. ______________ A financing instrument that conveys bare legal title on behalf of a beneficiary
7. ______________ A charge for the use of money
8. ______________ The act of charging interest in excess of the maximum legal rate
9. ______________ A charge imposed by lenders to adjust for the difference between interest rate and yield
10. ______________ The part of a financing agreement that gives the lender the right to declare the entire debt due and payable immediately on default

True or False

Circle the answer

1. T F A mortgage is classified as an involuntary lien on real estate.
2. T F A mortgage is a two-party financing agreement in which a mortgagee pledges real property to the mortgagor as security for the debt.
3. T F In title theory states, the mortgagor actually gives legal title to the mortgagee, while retaining equitable title.
4. T F When a property is mortgaged, the owner must execute both a promissory note and a security instrument.
5. T F The pledging of property as security for payment of a loan without actually surrendering possession of the property is referred to as subordination.
6. T F In a typical deed of trust, the mortgagee is the beneficiary and the borrower is the trustor.

Flash Cards (Pull out page & cut with scissors)

acceleration clause	hypothecation
alienation clause	interest
deed in lieu of foreclosure	mortgage, mortgagor, mortgagee
deed of trust	promissory note
deficiency judgment	satisfaction
discount point	usury

To pledge property as security for loan obligation without giving up possession of it; opposite of practice in a pawn shop

Chapter 14

Clause in mortgage or deed of trust that can be enforced to make the entire debt immediately if borrower defaults

Chapter 14

Charge made by lender for use of money; a charge to "rent" the money

Chapter 14

Also known as "due on sale" clause; permits lender to declare balance of loan immediately due if property is sold; prevents loan assumptions without lender approval

Chapter 14

Document creating a pledge of real estate as security for the payment of the debt; borrower is the mortgagor; lender is the mortgagee

Chapter 14

Way for mortgagor to avoid foreclosure by returning deed to lender/mortgagee

Chapter 14

Evidence that a loan was made; states terms of obligation, signed by its maker and is negotiable (transferable to a third party)

Chapter 14

Borrower conveys naked title to a trustee who holds it as security for the lender

Chapter 14

Also known as release; document indicating that the mortgage has been paid off

Chapter 14

Personal judgment levied against the borrower when a foreclosure sale does not produce sufficient funds to pay fully pay the mortgage debt

Chapter 14

Charging interest in excess of the maximum rate; often residential first mortgage loans are exempt from such laws

Chapter 14

Unit of measurement used for various loan charges; one point equals one percent of the loan amount

Chapter 14

True or False (Continued)

7\. T F A point is 1 percent of the purchase price of the property being offered as security for the loan.

8\. T F A defeasance clause expedites foreclosure by giving a lender the right to declare the entire debt due and payable in the event of a borrower's default.

9\. T F By provisions of a defeasance clause in most mortgage documents, the mortgagee is required to execute a satisfaction when the note has been fully paid, returning to the mortgagor all interest in the real estate.

10\. T F When a real estate loan secured by a deed of trust has been repaid in full, the beneficiary executes a discharge that releases the property back to the grantor.

11\. T F A buyer who purchases real property and assumes the seller's debt becomes personally obligated for the repayment of the entire debt.

12\. T F A mortgage or deed of trust must be recorded in the recorder's office of the county in which the real estate is located.

13\. T F In states that permit strict foreclosure, no sale of the property takes place.

14\. T F The right of a defaulted borrower to redeem his or her real estate within a certain period after the foreclosure sale is known as the statutory right of redemption.

15\. T F Usury is defined as the act of charging interest in excess of the maximum legal rate.

Multiple Choice

Circle A, B, C or D

1. States that recognize the lender as the "owner" of the mortgaged property are known as
   A. intermediate states.
   B. recordation theory states.
   C. title theory states.
   D. lien theory states.

2. A document that indicates that a loan has been made is referred to as a(n)
   A. promissory note.
   B. mortgage deed.
   C. deed of trust.
   D. satisfaction.

3. R defaults on her mortgage, and the lender forecloses. The lender's foreclosure suit is filed on March 15, and the sale is held on May 10. In R's state, a defaulted borrower is permitted to redeem his or her property within 60 days after the date of the sale. If R attempts to redeem the property on May 1, which of the following statements is true?
   A. R is exercising her statutory right of redemption.
   B. R is exercising her equitable right of redemption.
   C. R's attempt to redeem the property is too early; by statute, she must wait until after the sale.
   D. Under these facts, R cannot redeem the property.

4. A house is listed for $150,000. B buys it for $130,000 and makes a down payment of 20 percent. B borrows the balance on a fixed-rate mortgage at 6 percent. The lender charges four points. If there are no other closing costs involved, how much money should B bring to the closing?
   A. $4,160
   B. $16,000
   C. $26,000
   D. $30,160

5. P is a real estate broker. One afternoon, a client calls P at home. The client is obviously upset: "My lender just told me that my note and mortgage is a negotiable instrument!" the client says, voice shaking. "What does that mean?" Which of the following would be P's best response?
   A. "That's great! It means the lender is willing to negotiate on the interest rate."
   B. "Oh no! That means the mortgage can't be assumed by the next person you sell to."
   C. "Don't worry! That just means the mortgage can be sold by the lender."
   D. "Uh-oh! That means we have to go back to the sellers and ask them to pay the points."

Multiple Choice (Continued)

6. Deed of trust involves all of the following EXCEPT
   A. lender
   B. borrower
   C. trustee
   D. mortgagor

7. The state of West Oregon is a lien theory state. If N purchases Pineacre, and takes out a mortgage loan from K all of the following statements are true, EXCEPT
   A. N has retained both legal and equitable title to Pineacre.
   B. if N defaults on the loan, K must go through a formal foreclosure proceeding to recover the security.
   C. N has given legal title to K.
   D. K has only a lien interest in Pineacre.

8. Where a trust deed is used, the lender is the
   A. trustee.
   B. beneficiary.
   C. trustor.
   D. maker.

9. The Mortgage Company charges borrowers a 1.5 percent loan origination fee. T buys a house for $210,000 and pays $50,000 in cash. T applies for a mortgage to cover the balance. What will the Mortgage Company charge as a fee if the asking price of the house was $235,000?
   A. $2,400
   B. $3,150
   C. $3,525
   D. $3,750

10. A mortgage document contains the following clause: "In the event of Borrower's default under the terms of this Agreement, Lender may declare the entire unpaid balance of the debt due and payable immediately." This clause is referred to as a(n)
    A. hypothecation clause.
    B. acceleration clause.
    C. defeasance clause.
    D. release clause.

11. This month, H made the last payment on a mortgage loan secured by Blackacre. H's lender must execute a
    A. release deed.
    B. promissory note.
    C. possessory note.
    D. satisfaction of mortgage.

12. G took out a 15-year mortgage on Wetacre in 1992. On April 1, 1997, G's lender discovered that Wetacre lies in a flood hazard area as defined by the National Flood Insurance Reform Act of 1994. The lender informed G of the situation on April 15. Based on these facts, which of the following statements is true?
    A. The National Flood Insurance Reform Act of 1994 does not apply to G's property.
    B. G has until May 15 to purchase flood insurance.
    C. G has until May 30 to purchase flood insurance.
    D. If G refuses to purchase flood insurance, the lender must do so, but the lender may not charge the cost of the additional insurance to G.

13. J purchases Potter's Field from H for $45,000 in cash and assumes H's outstanding mortgage balance of $98,500. The lender executes a release for H. J fails to make any mortgage payments, and the lender forecloses. At the foreclosure sale, Potter's Field is sold for $75,000. Based on these facts, which of the following statements is true?
    A. H is solely liable for $23,500.
    B. J is solely liable for $23,500.
    C. J and H are equally liable for $23,500.
    D. J is solely liable for $30,000.

14. All of the following are true of a typical land contract EXCEPT
    A. At the end of the loan term, the seller will deliver clear title.
    B. The buyer is granted equitable title and possession.
    C. The vendee retains legal title during the contract term.
    D. In the event of a default, the vendor may retain any money already paid.

15. The borrower defaulted on his mortgage loan leaving an unpaid balance of $95,000. After receiving only $85,000 from the sale of the property, the lender filed for a
    A. lis pendens.
    B. release deed.
    C. satisfaction piece.
    D. deficiency judgment.

Multiple Choice (Continued)

16. B was the owner of Hasty Manor. When B defaulted on his loan, the trustee immediately sold Hasty Manor to recover the debt. The trustee acted under the terms of the security instrument. Based on these facts, which of the following statements is true?
    A. The exercise of this power of sale clause is an example of strict foreclosure.
    B. The trustee's sale of Hasty Manor was illegal, unless B's state permits such a so-called "friendly foreclosure."
    C. The exercise of this power of sale clause is an example of nonjudicial foreclosure.
    D. B could have exercised his statutory right of redemption at any time prior to the trustee's sale of Hasty Manor.

17. The difference between the interest rate that the lender charges and what the investor demands is made up by charging
    A. discount points.
    B. loan origination fees.
    C. satisfaction fees.
    D. underwriting fees.

18. What is the term that refers to a lender charging an interest rate that is higher than that permitted by law?
    A. Alienation
    B. Usury
    C. Hypothecation
    D. Defeasance

19. Parties to lending agreements are referred to by different terms. Which of the following refers to the same party?
    A. Borrower = Beneficiary
    B. Payor = Mortgagor
    C. Mortgagee = Borrower
    D. Trustor = Mortgagee

20. If the lender wants to call the entire note due and payable if the borrower stops making payments, the lender must include a(n)
    A. acceleration clause.
    B. defeasance clause.
    C. alienation clause.
    D. prepayment clause.

Redemption Rights Timeline

Figure 14.1

Write "Equitable" and "Statutory" in the appropriate "Right of Redemption" boxes below:

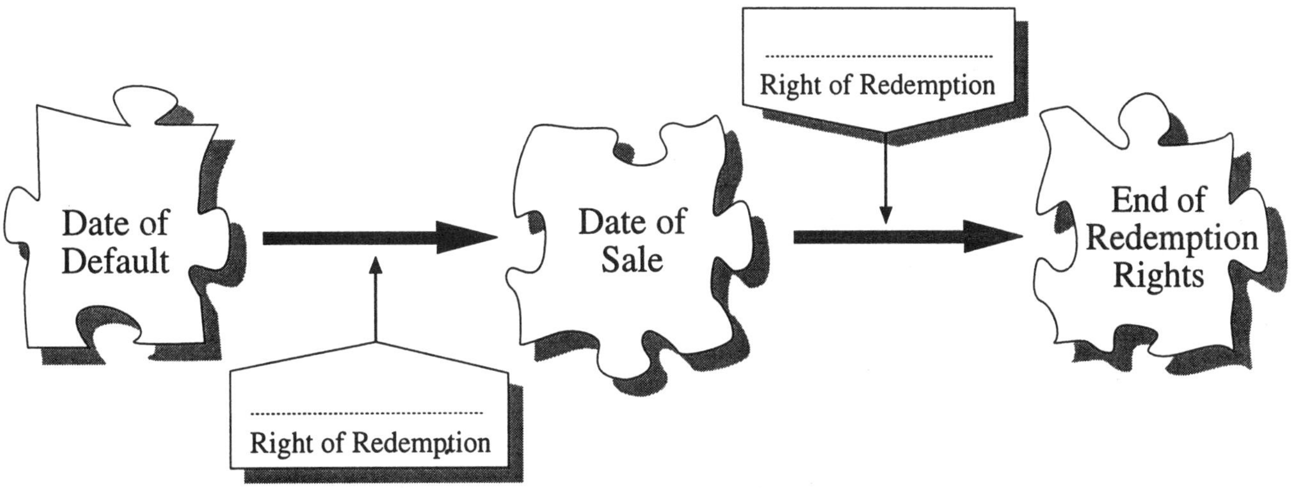

Matching (B)

Write the matching term on the appropriate line.

- alienation clause
- deed in lieu of foreclosure
- loan origination fee
- deficiency judgment
- equitable right of redemption
- foreclosure
- lien theory
- defeasance clause
- statutory right of redemption
- subordination agreement

1. ________________ Percentage of loan amount charged to borrower for costs of generating loan
2. ________________ The part of a financing agreement that requires the lender to execute a satisfaction or release when the note has been paid in full
3. ________________ A provision in a financing agreement that permits the lender to declare the entire debt due immediately in the event the property is sold
4. ________________ A device by which one lender agrees to change the priority of its loan relative to another lender
5. ________________ A legal procedure in which property pledged as security is sold to satisfy the debt
6. ________________ Property is transferred to the lender by mutual agreement rather than by legal action
7. ________________ A borrower's option of reinstating a defaulted debt prior to the foreclosure sale by paying the amount due
8. ________________ A right established by state law that permits a defaulted borrower to recover property within a limited time after a foreclosure sale
9. ________________ A procedure for obtaining the unpaid balance of a debt where the foreclosure sale does not generate sufficient funds
10. ________________ Idea that mortgage is purely a lien on real property

Answer Key

MATCHING (A)

1. mortgagor
2. mortgagee
3. execute
4. promissory note
5. hypothecation
6. deed of trust
7. interest
8. usury
9. discount points
10. acceleration clause

TRUE/FALSE ANSWERS

1. False A mortgage is classified as a voluntary lien on real estate.
2. False A mortgage is a two-party financing agreement in which a mortgagor pledges land to the mortgagee as security for the debt.
3. True
4. True
5. False The pledging of property as security for payment of a loan without actually surrendering possession of the property is referred to as hypothecation.

Answer Key (True or False - Continued)

6. True
7. False A point is one percent of the amount being borrowed.
8. False An acceleration clause expedites foreclosure by giving a lender the right to declare the entire debt due and payable in the event of a borrower's default.
9. True
10. False After a real estate loan, secured by a deed of trust, has been repaid in full, the trustee executes a release deed that releases the property back to the grantor.
11. True
12. True
13. True
14. True
15. True

MULTIPLE CHOICE ANSWERS

1. C Lien theory states feel that a mortgage is simply a lien on the property whereas title theory states interpret the a mortgage to mean that the lender is the owner of mortgaged land.
2. A The evidence that a loan has been made is found in the promissory note. A mortgage or deed of trust provides security for the loan. A satisfaction or release indicates that the loan has been repaid in full.
3. B R has an equity interest in the property until the foreclosure sale is complete; thus she is exercising her equitable right of redemption. In some states, she may retain a statutory right of redemption for a period of time after the foreclosure sale.
4. D \$130,000 x 20% = \$26,000 (down payment)
\$130,000 x 80% x 4% = \$4,160
\$26,000 + \$4,160 = \$30,160
5. C Negotiable instruments are transferable. A note and mortgage will often be sold on the secondary market.
6. D A mortgagor is the borrower in a mortgage. In a deed of trust, the borrower is the trustor and the trustee holds naked title in trust for the beneficiary (lender).
7. B This is a purchase money mortgage, a form of seller financing. When the mortgage is properly recorded, the former owner has to go through the same legal process that a lender would have to follow if there is a default.
8. B The trustor (borrower) conveys naked or bare title to the trustee who holds it in trust for the beneficiary (lender).
9. A The asking price is not relevant to this problem. \$210,000-\$50,000 x 1.5% = \$2,400
10. B Hypothecation is the act offering the property as security without giving up possession. The defeasance clause in a mortgage defeats the granting clause. A release indicates that the loan has been repaid in full.
11. D The promissory note shows that a loan was made. The satisfaction indicates that the loan was fully repaid. This is also sometimes called a release.
12. C If the lender discovers that that a secured property is in a flood hazard area, the borrower must be notified. The borrower has 45 days to purchase flood insurance. If the borrower does not buy the insurance, the lender must purchase the insurance and charge back the cost of the insurance to the borrower.
13. B Since the lender released the original borrower, the second borrower is fully responsible for the deficiency.
14. C The vendor retains legal title during the contract term in this form of seller financing.
15. D Lis pendens gives notice that the property is the subject of legal action. A satisfaction indicates that the loan was fully repaid. A deficiency results when the foreclosed property does not bring in enough money to fully repay the loan.

Answer Key (Continued)

16. C Strict foreclosure does not involve a sale. Proper notice is given to the delinquent borrower who is given time to make the payments. If they are not made, the court awards the property to the lender. A nonjudicial foreclosure does not involve the courts.

17. A Loan origination fees are charged to cover the cost of making the loan. The satisfaction indicates that the loan has been fully repaid.

18. B Hypothecation is giving property as security without giving up possession.

19. B The person who makes the payments to repay the loan is called the payor. The person who gave the property as security is called the mortgagor. Both are the same person: the borrower, the owner of the property.

20. A The acceleration clause permits the lender to declare the entire note due upon default by the borrower. The alienation clause is also known as the "due on sale" clause, permitting the lender to declare the entire note due if the property is sold, and thus prevents a loan assumption.

MATCHING (B)

1. loan origination fee
2. defeasance clause
3. alienation clause
4. subordination agreement
5. foreclosure
6. deed in lieu of foreclosure
7. equitable right of redemption
8. statutory right of redemption
9. deficiency judgment
10. lien theory

REDEMPTION RIGHTS TIMELINE (Figure 14.1)

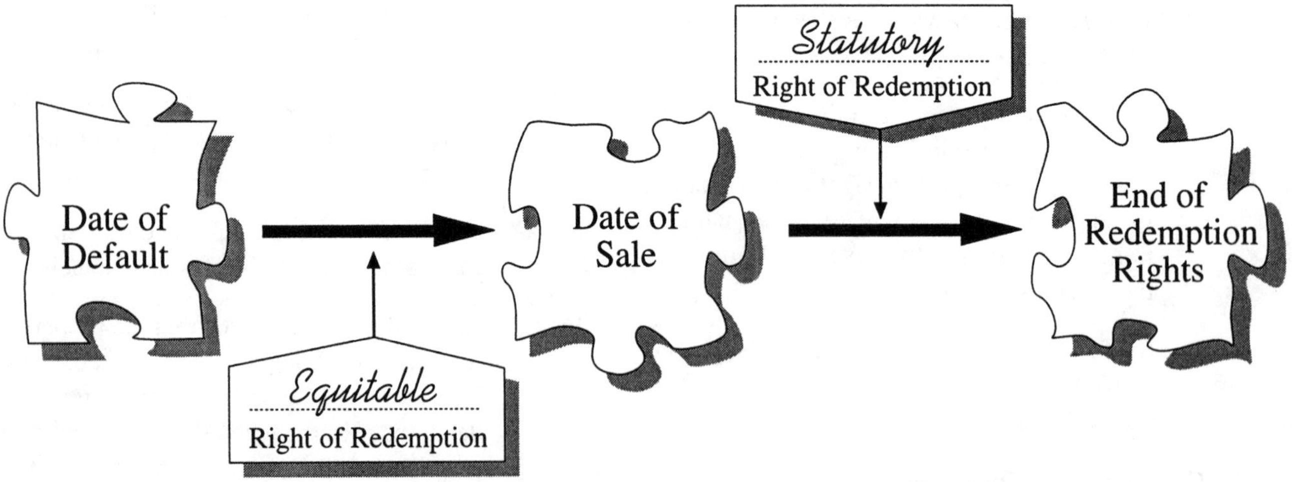

Real Estate Financing: Practice

15

Matching (A)

Write the matching term on the appropriate line.

- Federal Reserve
- amortized loan
- fiduciary lenders
- FNMA
- GNMA
- mortgage brokers
- secondary mortgage market
- prime rate
- primary mortgage market
- straight loan

1. ______________ A national system of banking districts designed to maintain sound credit conditions and a favorable economic climate
2. ______________ The short-term interest rate charged to a bank's largest, most creditworthy customers
3. ______________ Lenders who originate loans by making money available to borrowers
4. ______________ Thrifts, savings associations and commercial banks
5. ______________ Intermediaries who bring borrowers and lenders together
6. ______________ Investors who buy and sell loans after funding
7. ______________ A quasi-government agency organized as a private, stock-issuing corporation that buys pools of mortgages from lenders in exchange for mortgage-backed securities
8. ______________ A wholly governmental agency organized as a non-stock corporation that administers special assistance programs and participates in secondary market activities
9. ______________ A type of loan in which the borrower makes periodic interest payments, followed by the payment of the principal in full at the end of the term
10. ______________ A loan in which both principal and interest are paid off slowly, over time

True or False

Circle the answer

1. T F The Federal Reserve System is made up of the lenders who originate loans.

2. T F The discount rate is the short-term interest rate charged to a bank's largest, most creditworthy customers.

3. T F Income from a loan is generated by up-front finance charges collected at closings, plus interest collected during the loan term.

4. T F The primary mortgage market includes government agencies, insurance companies and mortgage bankers.

True or False (Continued)

5. T F The Federal National Mortgage Association ("Fannie Mae) is a privately owned corporation.

6. T F An amortized loan applies each monthly payment first toward the total interest owed over the life of the loan; once the total interest is paid off, each monthly payment is applied to the principal amount.

7. T F In an adjustable-rate mortgage, the interest rate is usually based on an objective economic indicator plus an additional premium, called a "margin."

8. T F In an adjustable-rate mortgage, the conversion option establishes how often the rate may be changed.

9. T F In a 20-year straight loan of $92,500 at 7 3/4 percent interest, the borrower's final payment will be $93,097.40.

10. T F The "value" portion of a property's LTV is the higher of the sale price or the appraised value.

11. T F The FHA is not a mortgage lender.

12. T F Unlike the FHA, the VA makes purchase-money loans to qualified individuals.

13. T F A wraparound loan covers more than one parcel or lot, and is usually used to finance subdivision developments.

14. T F In an open-end loan, the interest rate on the initial amount borrowed is fixed, but the rate on future advances is linked to future market rates.

15. T F Under Regulation Z, consumers must be fully informed of all finance charges, and the true interest rate, prior to the completion of a transaction.

16. T F Under the Equal Credit Opportunity Act, a residential purchase-money borrower has three days in which to rescind a transaction simply by notifying the lender of his or her intent to rescind.

17. T F Under the Community Reinvestment Act, the findings of the government agency review of an institution's reinvestment activities are strictly confidential.

18. T F A computerized loan origination system allows a real estate broker to select a lender and apply for a loan on a buyer's behalf.

19. T F A VA appraisal is referred to as a certificate of reasonable value (CRV).

20. T F Under Truth-in-Lending law, a phrase such as "no money down" triggers certain disclosures.

Multiple Choice

Circle A, B, C or D

1. All of the following are roles of the Federal Reserve System EXCEPT
   A. help counteract inflationary trends.
   B. create a favorable economic climate.
   C. maintain sound credit conditions.
   D. make direct loans to buyers.

2. A lender who collects payments, processes them and follows up on loan delinquencies is said to
   A. increase the yield to the lender.
   B. service the loan.
   C. insure loan payments.
   D. underwrite the loans.

adjustable rate mortgage (ARM)	loan-to-value ratio
amortized loan	primary mortgage market
Equal Credit Opportunity Act (ECOA)	private mortgage insurance
Federal Home Loan Mortgage Corporation	Real Estate Settlement ProceduresAct (RESPA)
Fannie Mae	Regulation Z
Ginnie Mae	Truth-in-Lending Act

Relationship between amount of mortgage loan and value of the real estate being pledged as collateral

Chapter 15

Loan that has a fluctuating interest rate, usually one tied to a cost-of-funds index; the cost of doing business is the margin that stays fixed and is added to the base rate

Chapter 15

Mortgage market in which loans are originated; includes commercial banks, savings banks, mutual banks; the market that meets borrowers face-to-face

Chapter 15

Loan in which the monthly payment consists of principal and interest that partially pay off both each month over the term of the loan

Chapter 15

PMI; insurance provided by private carrier that protects a lender against loss if a foreclosure and deficiency; usually insures top 10-20 percent of the loan

Chapter 15

Federal law that prohibits discrimination in the extension of credit because of race, color, religion, national origin, sex, receipt of public assistance, age, marital status

Chapter 15

Federal law requires certain disclosures to consumers about mortgage loan closings; prohibits kickbacks, certain referral fees, requires good faith estimate in 3 business days

Chapter 15

Corporation buys primarily conventional mortgage loans in secondary market; does not guarantee principal and interest payments of these mortgages

Chapter 15

Implements Truth-in-Lending Act requiring credit institutions to inform borrowers of true cost of obtaining a loan (APR); certain advertising "triggers" disclosures in ads

Chapter 15

Quasi-government agency buys any kind of mortgage loans in secondary market from primary lenders; guarantees timely principal and interest to security holders

Chapter 15

Consumer protection act intended to force lenders to be truthful in their advertising; implemented by Regulation Z

Chapter 15

HUD division, corporation without stock; administers special-assistance programs and works in tandem with Fannie Mae by guaranteeing payments

Chapter 15

Flash Cards (Pull out page & cut with scissors)

balloon payment	purchase-money mortgage
blanket loan	reverse-annuity mortgage (RAM)
conventional loan	sale-leaseback
Federal Reserve System	secondary mortgage market
FHA loan	straight loan
package loan	VA loan

Form of seller financing; note and mortgage from buyer are given to seller (lender) as part of the purchase price of the real estate

Chapter 15

Final payment of mortgage loan that is considerably larger than the required periodic payments because the loan amount was not fully amortized

Chapter 15

RAM; homeowner receives monthly payments based on accumulated equity rather than one lump sum; repaid at certain date or owner's death or sale of property

Chapter 15

Mortgage loan secured by more than one parcel of real estate, provides for each parcel's partial release from mortgage lien upon some repayment; used by developers

Chapter 15

Transaction in which owner sells improved property and as part of transaction, signs a long-term lease to remain in possession of premises; permits owner to "pull out" equity

Chapter 15

Loan that is neither FHA nor VA; does not require insurance or guarantee, although today high LTV loans are made along with PMI (private mortgage insurance)

Chapter 15

Market for purchase and sale of existing mortgages; designed to provide greater liquidity for mortgages; generally does not deal directly with borrowers

Chapter 15

Country's central banking system; responsible for nation's monetary policy by regulating supply of money and interest rates; requires member banks to keep a reserve

Chapter 15

Loan in which only interest is paid during term of loan with entire principal amount due with the final interest payment

Chapter 15

Loan insured by Federal Housing Administration; made by approved lender with FHA's regulations; borrower pays mortgage insurance premium (MIP)

Chapter 15

Mortgage to qualified veteran by authorized lender; guaranteed by Dept. of Veteran Affairs; up to 100% LTV based on certificate of reasonable value (CRV)

Chapter 15

Real estate loan secured by both real and personal property; i.e., new home that includes window treatments and major appliances

Chapter 15

Multiple Choice (Continued)

3. Which of the following is a more risky investment because it does not guarantee payments?
   A. Freddie Mac
   B. Fannie Mae
   C. Ginnie Mae
   D. FDIC

4. Name the kind of loan in which the interest rate is tied to the movement of an objective economic indicator.
   A. Buydown
   B. Graduated mortgage payment
   C. Adjustable rate mortgage
   D. Straight loan

5. The loan in which equal payments reduce the full amount of principal and interest to zero is a(n)
   A. hypothecation.
   B. straight loan.
   C. amortized loan.
   D. buydown.

6. The borrower who chooses an adjustable rate mortgage can depend on the margin to
   A. remain constant for the life of the loan.
   B. fluctuate according to some economic index.
   C. only change according to an agreed upon amount.
   D. decrease over the life of the loan.

7. To qualify for an FHA-insured loan, the borrower's monthly housing expenses and total other monthly obligations cannot exceed what percent of his or her total gross monthly income?
   A. 28 percent
   B. 36 percent
   C. 41 percent
   D. Varies according to the loan amount

8. What does private mortgage insurance cover?
   A. Pays the lender if the borrower dies
   B. Reimburses the lender if the borrower defaults
   C. Protects the top 25 to 30 percent of the loan against borrower default
   D. Pays the borrower if the borrower loses the house to a title claim

9. Regulation Z always applies to
   A. a credit transaction secured by a residence.
   B. business loans.
   C. commercial loans.
   D. agricultural loans of more than $25,000.

10. Who is responsible for paying the broker or her salesperson when one of them takes the loan application from a borrower?
    A. Lender
    B. Borrower
    C. Seller
    D. Split between the lender and borrower

11. K's monthly mortgage payment is $520. The interest rate on the loan is 10 percent, and the outstanding balance is $43,500. When K makes this month's payment, what amount of the total payment will be applied to interest, and what amount to principal?
    A. $362.50 interest; $157.50 principal
    B. $435.00 interest; $85.00 principal
    C. $520.00 interest; $0 principal
    D. $85.00 interest; $435.00 principal

12. All of the following are true regarding the Federal Reserve System, EXCEPT
    A. all federally chartered banks must join the Federal Reserve System and purchase stock in its district reserve banks.
    B. the Federal Reserve requires that member banks set aside assets as reserve funds for use exclusively as mortgage loans.
    C. by increasing or decreasing reserve requirements, the Federal Reserve controls the amount of money available for mortgage loans.
    D. member banks are permitted to borrow money from the reserve banks to expand their local banking operations.

13. All of the following are lenders in the primary mortgage market, EXCEPT
    A. endowment funds.
    B. mortgage brokers.
    C. insurance companies.
    D. credit unions.

14. If a buyer obtains a loan for $13,500, and the interest rate is 7 1/2 percent, what is the amount of semiannual interest payable?
    A. $457.14
    B. $506.25
    C. $596.55
    D. $602.62

15. A house had a sales price of $80,000. The buyer obtained a loan for $72,000. If the lender charges three points, what will the buyer pay?
    A. $1,980
    B. $2,160
    C. $2,420
    D. $2,610

Multiple Choice (Continued)

16. Last month, M's total mortgage payment included $412.50 in interest on a loan with an outstanding balance of $60,000. What is M's annual rate of interest?
    A. 7 1/2 percent
    B. 7 3/4 percent
    C. 8 1/4 percent
    D. 8 1/2 percent

17. Under the terms of B's adjustable-rate mortgage, the interest rate B must pay is (1) the U.S. Treasury bill rate as of June 1 of each year, not to exceed 8.95 percent for any period; plus (2) 1.5 percent. What is the term used to describe (2)?
    A. rate cap
    B. index
    C. margin
    D. payment cap

18. G bought a cottage overlooking the ocean. The asking price for the cottage was $85,000; G offered $83,550 and the seller accepted. The appraised value of the cottage is $82,000. G plans to pay $15,000 in cash and take out a mortgage for the remainder. What is the LTV for this property?
    A. 80 percent
    B. 82 percent
    C. 84 percent
    D. 89 percent

19. A borrower took out an FHA-insured loan on a single-family home on August 1, 1995. If the borrower wishes to prepay the loan, which of the following statements is true?
    A. The borrower must give the lender 30 day written notice of his or her intent to prepay and may be charged a penalty of one month's interest.
    B. If the borrower fails to give the lender 30 days' written notice of his or her intent to prepay, the lender has the option of charging a penalty of up to 30 days' interest.
    C. No written notice is required, but lenders are permitted to charge a reasonable prepayment penalty.
    D. No written notice is required and there is no prepayment penalty.

20. P is buying Hilltop House from R. R bought Hilltop House on December 14, 1989, with an FHA loan and has lived there ever since. Because of its favorable terms, P would like to assume R's mortgage. Is this possible?
    A. Yes; there are no restrictions on the assumption of this mortgage.
    B. Yes, but P will have to go through the complete buyer qualification process.
    C. Yes, but P will have to undergo a creditworthiness review.
    D. No; this FHA loan is unassumable.

21. In 1967, R served for six months on active duty in Vietnam. After winning a medal for bravery and being honorably discharged, R went back to college, received a degree in engineering and went to work for a large construction company. In 1993, R was killed in a tragic skiing accident. R's widow wishes to use R's life insurance money to make a down payment on a condominium and believes she is entitled to a VA-guaranteed loan. Is she correct?
    A. Yes; the unremarried spouse of a qualified veteran is entitled to a VA-guaranteed loan.
    B. Yes; whether or not she remarries, R's widow is entitled to the same VA benefits as R was during his life.
    C. No; R's death was not service-related.
    D. No; R did not meet the time-in-service criteria for qualified veterans.

22. Which of the following makes direct loans to qualified borrowers?
    A. VA
    B. FSA
    C. Fannie Mae
    D. FHA

23. K is purchasing a fully furnished condominium unit. In this situation, K would be most likely to use a
    A. package loan.
    B. blanket loan.
    C. wraparound loan.
    D. buydown.

24. G, a real estate broker, has a CLO terminal in her office. Because there are more than a dozen lending institutions in the city, G has found that the CLO greatly streamlines the application process for her clients. G sits down at the terminal with B, a homebuyer, and the following events take place
    (1) G explains that there is a fee for using the terminal of one-half point, based on the loan amount, and that B may choose to finance the fee;
    (2) G explains the different kinds of services offered by the two local lenders who pay G a monthly "screen fee," to be included on the CLO system;
    (3) G helps B answer the on-screen qualification questions.

    Which of these events is an improper use of a CLO system?
    A. 1 only
    B. 2 only
    C. 2 and 3
    D. 1 and 3

Multiple Choice (Continued)

25. The Equal Credit Opportunity Act prohibits lenders from discriminating against credit applicants on the basis of all of the following factors, EXCEPT

   A. religion.
   B. past credit history.
   C. income from public assistance.
   D. marital status.

Matching (B)

Write the matching term on the appropriate line.

- blanket loan
- adjustable rate mortgage
- buydown
- certificate of eligibility
- Equal Credit Opportunity Act
- package loan
- growing equity mortgage
- purchase money mortgage
- Truth-in-Lending
- Real Estate Settlement Procedures Act

1. ________________ A form of loan in which the interest rate fluctuates depending on the behavior of an objective economic index
2. ________________ A fixed interest-rate mortgage in which payments of principal are increased over the term according to an index or schedule
3. ________________ The document that determines the maximum guarantee to which a veteran is entitled
4. ________________ Form of seller financing whereby the buyer gives the seller a note and mortgage
5. ________________ A loan that includes both real and personal property
6. ________________ A method of financing the purchase of property that temporarily lowers the initial interest rate through the payment of a lump sum of cash to the lender
7. ________________ Lending law prohibiting discrimination based on marital status or sex
8. ________________ Type of mortgage used by developers, securing the loan with several parcels
9. ________________ Law that prohibits kickbacks
10. ________________ Law that requires lenders to reveal the true cost of borrowing money

Math Practice

Calculate the Answers

Use the Loan Table in Figure 15.1 to solve the five problems below.

Figure 15.1

Amortized Loans

(Monthly Payments per $1,000 of Loan Principal)

Annual Int. Rate	Life of Loan 5 yrs	10 yrs	15 yrs	20 yrs	25 yrs	30 yrs	35 yrs	40 yrs
5.00%	$18.87	$10.61	$7.91	$6.60	$5.85	$5.37	$5.05	$4.82
5.50%	19.10	10.85	8.17	6.88	6.14	5.68	5.37	5.16
6.00%	19.33	11.10	8.44	7.16	6.44	6.00	5.70	5.50
6.50%	19.57	11.35	8.71	7.46	6.75	6.32	6.04	5.85
7.00%	19.80	11.61	8.99	7.75	7.07	6.65	6.39	6.21
7.50%	20.04	11.87	9.27	8.06	7.39	6.99	6.74	6.58
8.00%	20.28	12.13	9.56	8.36	7.72	7.34	7.10	6.95
8.50%	20.52	12.40	9.85	8.68	8.05	7.69	7.47	7.33
9.00%	20.76	12.67	10.14	9.00	8.39	8.05	7.84	7.71
9.50%	21.00	12.94	10.44	9.32	8.74	8.41	8.22	8.10
10.00%	21.25	13.22	10.75	9.65	9.09	8.78	8.60	8.49
10.50%	21.49	13.49	11.05	9.98	9.44	9.15	8.98	8.89
11.00%	21.74	13.78	11.37	10.32	9.80	9.52	9.37	9.28

1. The borrower wants to borrow $125,000 for 20 years. He will pay 8.5 percent interest. What will his monthly principal and interest payments be? What will be the cost of interest over the life of the loan?

2. A single woman wants to borrow $135,600 to buy a house. If she must pay 9 percent annual interest, and she can afford a monthly payment of $1,100 (principal and interest), what is the lowest number of years she can borrow the money?

3. A couple plans to borrow $75,000 to buy their first home. If they can find mortgage money at 7.5 percent instead of 9 percent for a 30-year loan, how much lower will their principal and interest payments be?

4. K can afford $1,175 per month for a payment that includes principal, interest, taxes and insurance. Annual property taxes are $840 and insurance will cost $480 per year. If current interest rates are at 7 percent, and K wants a 30-year loan, how much can he afford to borrow?

5. The borrower wants a 15-year mortgage instead of the typical 30-year mortgage. He will be borrowing $95,000 at 6.5 percent. How much more will this cost each month? How much will he save in interest payments over the life of the loan?

ANSWERS:

1. ______________
2. ______________
3. ______________
4. ______________
5. ______________

Math Practice (Continued)

Carlos and Wendy have just purchased a house for $92,000. They are looking for a 30-year loan and have been quoted an interest rate of 8 percent. Now they are trying to decide if they should obtain an 80 percent conventional loan, a 90 percent conventional loan or an FHA-insured loan or use Wendy's VA eligibility to obtain a VA-guaranteed loan.

To help Carlos and Wendy make a decision, fill in the table in Figure 15.2.

(Use the mortgage rate factor of $7.34/$1,000 of loan amount to determine the principal and interest per month; ignore the effect of closing costs.)

Figure 15.2

TYPE OF LOAN	PURCHASE PRICE	MAXIMUM LOAN	DOWN PAYMENT	P & I Per MONTH
80% Conventional	$92,000			
90% Conventional	$92,000			
FHA	$92,000			
VA	$92,000			

Answer Key

MATCHING (A)

1. Federal Reserve
2. prime rate
3. primary mortgage market
4. fiduciary lenders
5. mortgage brokers
6. secondary mortgage market
7. FNMA
8. GNMA
9. straight loan
10. amortized loan

TRUE OR FALSE

1. False — The primary mortgage market is made up of the lenders who originate loans.
2. False — The prime rate is the short-term interest rate charged to a bank's largest, most creditworthy customers.
3. True
4. True
5. True
6. False — An amortized loan applies each payment first toward the interest owed on the loan; the remainder of each payment is then applied toward paying off the principal amount.
7. True
8. False — In an adjustable rate mortgage, the adjustment period establishes how often the rate may be changed.
9. True
10. False — The "value" portion of a property's LTV is the lower of the sale price or the appraised value.
11. True
12. False — Like the FHA, the VA does not make purchase-money loans to qualified individuals.
13. False — A blanket loan covers more than one parcel or lot, and is usually used to finance subdivision developments.
14. True
15. True

Answer Key (Continued)

16. False Under Regulation Z, a borrower other than a residential purchase-money or first mortgage borrower has three days in which to rescind a transaction simply by notifying the lender of his or her intent to rescind.

17. False Under the Community Reinvestment Act, the findings of the government agency review of an institution's community reinvestment activities must be made public.

18. False A computerized loan origination system allows a real estate broker to assist a buyer in selecting a lender and applying for a loan.

19. True

20. True

MULTIPLE CHOICE ANSWERS

1. D The Federal Reserve does not make direct loans to consumers.

2. B Discount points increase the yield to the lender; underwriting is matching an investor to a borrower; mortgage insurance insures the lender against borrower default.

3. A Fannie Mae guarantees interest and principal payments to the holder of FNMA securities and Ginnie Mae guarantees payments and absorbs the difference between the low yield and current market prices. Freddie Mac does neither.

4. C A graduated mortgage payment begins below market rate and increases each year for several years. A lump sum payment to the lender reduces the monthly payment, called a buydown. A borrower makes interest only payments and one final principal payment when using a straight loan.

5. C The payment is first credited to the interest owed, and the remainder applied to reduce the principal.

6. A The margin remains constant during the life of the loan; the interest rate tied to the index fluctuates as the index fluctuates.

7. C The FHA borrower's long term debts and housing costs may add up to 41 percent of gross monthly income. The same costs may total only 36 percent for most conventional loans.

8. C Private mortgage insurance, usually required for loans more than 80 percent of value, provides security to the lender if the borrower defaults.

9. A The truth-in-lending law, implemented by Regulation Z does not apply to commercial, business or agricultural loans of more than $25,000.

10. B The borrower who uses a computerized loan originator must pay the fee to the broker or salesperson who takes the application.

11. A $43,500 x 10% ÷ 12 = $362.50 monthly interest ($520 - $362.50 = $157.50)

12. B The Federal Reserve requires that member banks set aside reserve funds that cannot be used for loans or any other use.

13. B Mortgage brokers do not loan their own money; they are intermediaries who bring borrowers and lenders together.

14. B $13,500 x 7.5% ÷ 2 = $506.25

15. B Points are charged on the loan amount, not the sale price. $72,000 x 3% = $2,160

16. C The monthly interest must be annualized in order to calculate the interest rate.

$412.50 x 12 ÷ $60,000 = 8.25 percent

17. C The rate set by the U. S. Treasury bill rate is the index in the adjustable rate mortgage. The cost of doing business is the margin which remains constant during the life of the loan and is added to the Treasury bill rate.

18. C LTV = Loan Amt ÷ Appraised Value of Sale Price (whichever is lower), thus:

$83,550 - $15,000 = $68,550 ÷ $82,000 = 84 %

Multiple Choice (Continued)

19. D For FHA loans taken out before 1985, the lender has the option of charging a prepayment penalty if the borrower pays off the loan without giving at least a 30-day notice. However, since August 2, 1985, no written notice is required.

20. C FHA loans made before December 1986 are freely assumable. Those made between December 1, 1986 and December 15, 1989, a credit worthiness review of the prospective assumer is required. If the loan had been made just a couple of days later, no assumptions are permitted without complete buyer qualification.

21. C The widow of a serviceman whose death is service-related may use his entitlements. In this situation, she is not entitled.

22. B The Farm Service Agency will guarantee loans made and serviced by private lenders and guaranteed for a specific percentage; the FSA will also make loans directly to the borrower.

23. A A loan secured by a fully furnished condominium unit is secured by both real and personal property. A blanket loan is secured by several properties.

24. B Consumers must be informed of the availability of other lenders.

25. B Lenders may definitely decide to not make a loan because of the borrower's previous credit history. Otherwise, lenders may not discriminate on the basis of race, color, religion, national origin, sex, receipt of public assistance, age or marital status.

MATCHING (B)

1. adjustable rate mortgage
2. growing equity mortgage
3. certificate of eligibility
4. purchase money mortgage
5. package loan
6. buydown
7. Equal Credit Opportunity Act
8. blanket loan
9. Real Estate Settlement Procedures Act
10. Truth-in-Lending

AMORTIZATION TABLE ANSWERS

1. \$125,000 ÷ 1,000 x 8.68 = \$1,085 monthly P&I x 240 = \$260,400 - \$125,000 = \$135,400 interest over the life of the loan

2. \$135,600 ÷ 1000 = 135.6
   \$1100 ÷ 135.6 = 8.11 which is the factor for 9 percent at 30 years

3. at 9 percent 75 x 8.05 = \$603.75
   at 7.5 percent 75 x 6.99 = \$524.25
   \$603.75 - \$524.25 = \$79.50 lower each month

4. \$840 ÷ 12 = \$70; \$480 ÷ 12 = \$40
   \$1175 - \$70 - \$40 = \$1,065 ÷ 6.65 x 1000 = \$160,150 (maximum loan amount)

5. The borrower will have to pay \$227.05 more each month with the 15-year loan, but will save \$67,203 in interest over the life of the loan
   15-yr 95 x 8.71 = \$827.45 x 15 x 12 = \$148,941
   30-yr 95 x 6.32 = \$600.40 x 30 x 12 = \$216,144

Figure 15.2

TYPE OF LOAN	PURCHASE PRICE	MAXIMUM LOAN	DOWN PAYMENT	P & I Per MONTH
80% Conventional	\$92,000	73,600	18,400	540.22
90% Conventional	\$92,000	82,800	9,200	607.75
FHA	\$92,000	87,900	4,100	645.00
VA	\$92,000	92,000	0	675.28

16 Leases

Matching

Write the matching term on the appropriate line.

- actual eviction
- constructive eviction
- tenancy at will
- option
- periodic tenancy
- reversionary right
- sublease
- lease
- tenancy for years
- tenancy at sufferance

1. ______________ A contract between a real estate owner and a tenant
2. ______________ A landlord's right to possession of the premises after the expiration of the lease term
3. ______________ A leasehold estate that has a specific beginning and a definite end
4. ______________ The estate created when a landlord and tenant enter into an agreement that automatically renews
5. ______________ A leasehold estate with an indefinite term that may be terminated by the death of either the landlord or tenant
6. ______________ The leasehold estate created when a tenant who was in lawful possession of real property continues in possession without the landlord's consent
7. ______________ The transfer of some of a tenant's interests, but not his or her obligations
8. ______________ A lessee's privilege of renewing a lease
9. ______________ The process by which a landlord regains possession of leased premises following a tenant's breach
10. ______________ The action by which a tenant may properly abandon premises that have become unusable due to the landlord's conscious neglect

True or False

Circle the answer

1. T F In a lease agreement, the landlord is the lessee and the tenant is the lessor.
2. T F Unlike a freehold estate, a leasehold estate is considered personal property.
3. T F The main difference between a tenancy at will and a tenancy at sufferance is the landlord's consent.
4. T F Although an extension of a tenancy for years requires a new contract, the lease may be terminated prior to the expiration date by either party at any time.
5. T F Periodic tenancies are characterized by continuity because they are automatically renewable.

Flash Cards (Pull out page & cut with scissors)

assignment	**gross lease**
constructive eviction	**lease, lessor, lessee**
estate at sufferance	**leasehold estate**
estate at will	**lease purchase**
estate for years	**net lease**
estate from period to period	**percentage lease**

Tenant pays rent, landlord pays all expenses of property; most common form or residential lease

Chapter 16

In a lease, transferring all of one's remaining interest in the property, although the original lessee is still responsible for the financial obligations

Chapter 16

Contract (lease) between landlord (lessor) who gives up possession and tenant (lessee) who pays rent

Chapter 16

When the tenant is forced to vacate the property because the landlord failed to provide essential services; tenant is no longer obligated for any further rent

Chapter 16

Tenant's right to occupy real estate during term of lease, generally held to be a personal property interest

Chapter 16

Tenant remains on the property, without the landlord's permission, after the lease has expired

Chapter 16

Purchase of real property after a period of a lease, usually long-term; usually done for tax or financing purposes

Chapter 16

Term is indefinite; i.e., "I will rent to you until I sell the house;" will be terminated by death of either party or sale of property

Chapter 16

Lease requiring tenant to pay not only rent but also taxes, insurance, utilities and repairs

Chapter 16

Leasehold interest for specific period of time; definite beginning, definite ending; not terminated by death of either party, nor sale of property; no notice required

Chapter 16

Common lease for retail property; often a base monthly rent plus a percentage of any gross sales over that amount

Chapter 16

Leasehold interest that automatically renews until either party gives notice to change the terms; month-to-month; not terminated by death of either party, nor sale of property

Chapter 16

True or False (Continued)

6. T F The elements of a valid lease are (1) offer and acceptance, (2) capacity of the parties, (3) consideration, and (4) legal objective.

7. T F The covenant of quiet enjoyment is a guarantee by the landlord that the tenant is entitled to a quiet building without interference from noisy neighbors.

8. T F A tenant who is leasing only a part of a building is not required to continue paying rent if the leased premises are destroyed.

9. T F When a tenant transfers all of his or her leasehold interests to another person, he or she has assigned the lease.

10. T F Under a net lease agreement, the landlord pays all the operating expenses of the property, while the tenant pays only a fixed rental.

11. T F Ground leases are generally short-term net leases.

12. T F Except in the case of a tenancy at will or a lease from the owner of a life estate, the death of one of the parties does not terminate the lease.

13. T F To be entitled to constructive eviction, the tenant must show only that the premises have become unusable for the purpose stated in the lease.

14. T F The Fair Housing Amendments Act of 1988 requires that, in leased housing, the same criteria must be applied to tenants with children as are applied to adults.

15. T F All leases must require a security deposit as part of the consideration.

Multiple Choice

Circle A, B, C or D

1. The tenant pays for his own utilities and makes one payment each month to the landlord who takes care of the taxes, insurance on the building and maintenance. What type of lease arrangement is this?
   A. Net
   B. Gross
   C. Percentage
   D. Graduated

2. Tenants want to buy the house they are renting. However, they do not have enough money for the down payment. The landlord agreed to put part of the tenants' rent towards the purchase price. The landlord and tenants have agreed to a(n)
   A. lease purchase.
   B. sale leaseback.
   C. ground lease.
   D. option.

3. The expiration date of the lease is September 30. On July 1, the house is sold to a family that wants to live in the rental property. How soon can they move in?
   A. July 1, present year
   B. July 1, next year
   C. October 1, present year
   D. December 31, present year

4. N rents an apartment from R under a one-year written lease. The expiration date of the lease is May 1. How much notice must R give N to recover possession on May 1?
   A. 30 days
   B. 60 days
   C. One week
   D. No notice is required

5. In 1992, M rented Brownacre to N. The agreement stated only that N agreed to pay M $500 per month. What type of tenancy does N have?
   A. Holdover
   B. At sufferance
   C. For years
   D. Periodic

6. S rents an apartment under a two-year written lease from C. Three months after signing the lease, S is transferred to another country for a year. During this period, S leases the apartment to J. J mails monthly rent checks to S, who continues making monthly rental payments to C. In this situation, J has a
   A. lease.
   B. tenancy at will.
   C. sublease.
   D. periodic tenancy.

Multiple Choice (Continued)

7. F lives in an apartment building owned by H. On a Monday during a particularly hot August, vandals break into the building and destroy the central air-conditioning system. F's apartment becomes uncomfortably warm. On Tuesday, F sues H for constructive eviction. Under these facts, will F win?
   A. Yes, if F's lease promises that the apartment will be air conditioned.
   B. Yes; to claim constructive eviction, it is not necessary that the condition be the result of the landlord's personal actions.
   C. No; to claim constructive eviction, the tenant must prove that the premises are uninhabitable.
   D. No; the premises are not unusable, the condition was not due to H's conscious neglect and F has not abandoned the apartment.

8. V is a tenant in Bountiful Towers under a one-year lease signed in August. Rent payments are due on the 15th of each month. On December 12, Bountiful Towers is sold to a new owner. On March 14, the building burns to the ground. Which of the following statements accurately describes V's obligations?
   A. V is not required to continue paying rent after March 14, because the premises have been destroyed.
   B. V is not required to continue paying rent after December 12, because the sale voids the preexisting lease.
   C. V is required to continue paying rent for the full lease term, because a tenancy for years cannot be terminated by the destruction of the premises.
   D. V is required to continue paying rent, but the residential lease is converted by law into a ground lease.

9. J signs a lease to rent an apartment. J's lease runs from October 1 until November 1 of the following year. K signs a one-year lease to rent an apartment in a new high-rise building that will be ready for occupancy in 15 months. Which of these leases must be in writing to satisfy the statute of frauds?
   A. J's only
   B. K's only
   C. Both J's and K's
   D. Neither J's nor K's

10. A tenant signed a one-year lease with a landlord on April 10, 1997. On March 1, 1998, the landlord asked the tenant whether the lease would be renewed. The tenant did not respond, but was still in the apartment on April 11, 1998. What can the landlord do?
    A. The landlord must initiate eviction proceedings within the first one- month rental period.
    B. The landlord cannot evict the tenant; because the tenant remained in possession of the premises, the lease has been automatically renewed for an additional year.
    C. If the landlord accepts a rent check, the tenant is entitled to a renewal of the one-year lease.
    D. The landlord may either evict the holdover tenant or accept a rent check, creating a periodic tenancy.

11. If a tenant remains in possession of leased property after the expiration of the lease term, without paying rent and without the landlord's consent, what is his or her status?
    A. Tenant at will
    B. Tenant at sufferance
    C. Periodic tenant
    D. Freehold tenant

12. J wanted to rent an apartment from K. Because of a physical disability, it would be necessary for J to have all the doorknobs and light switches in the unit lowered to a height of 12 inches from the floor. This would require the installation of new doors and locks, custom-made appliances and the complete rewiring of both J's unit and several neighboring apartments. In addition, the floors in J's unit would have to be reinforced by installing steel beams and posts in the apartment beneath and in the basement. Based on these facts, which of the following statements is true?
    A. The Fair Housing Act requires that K make the accommodation for J at K's expense; no additional rent may be charged for J's modified unit.
    B. If the modifications demanded by J are not reasonable, K is not legally required to permit them.
    C. Regardless of the nature of the modifications, J's access right is protected by the Americans with Disabilities Act, and K is legally obligated to permit the modifications to be made at J's expense.
    D. Because the proposed modifications would interfere with a future tenant's use of the premises, K may refuse to permit them.

Multiple Choice (Continued)

13. N operates a small store in a shopping center. Under the terms of the lease, the landlord pays all operating expenses. N pays a base rent of $1,000 per month, plus 15 percent of monthly gross profits over $10,000. N has a
    A. gross lease.
    B. percentage lease.
    C. net lease.
    D. variable lease.

14. When a landowner leases unimproved land to a tenant, who agrees to erect a building on the land, the lease is usually referred to as a(n)
    A. lease purchase.
    B. gross lease.
    C. ground lease.
    D. improvement lease.

15. G rented a house from R. During the lease term, G had to move out of state. G assigned the lease to P, who failed to make any rental payments. In this situation, which of the following statements is true?
    A. G has no obligation to R, because the lease was assigned, not sublet.
    B. P has no obligation to R, because P's lease agreement is with G.
    C. G is still liable to R for the outstanding rent, since R did not release G when the lease was assigned to P.
    D. G is still liable to R, because G's arrangement with P as described is a sublease, not an assignment.

Types of Commercial Leases

Figure 16.1 shows part of the Happy Shoppers Mall in the exclusive suburban community of West Flightpath. Based on the information given below, write the type of lease and current month's rental beneath each store.

1. Acrylic Acres pays a base rent of $1,500 per month and 15 percent of property charges, limited to utilities and taxes. Blue Buttons Boutique pays a base rent of $2,000 per month and no property charges. Custom Custards pays a base rent of $1,850 per month and no property charges, but pays 12 percent of its monthly gross sales over $4,000 to the landlord.

2. Acrylic Acres earned $10,000 in gross profits and netted $4,850. Blue Buttons Boutique grossed $6,500 and earned a net profit of $3,000. Custom Custards had a gross income of $9,542, with profits after expenses of $7,370 for the month.

3. This month, the Happy Shoppers Mall had to pay $6,790 in utility bills and $495 in regular repairs and maintenance. The month's prorated share of local property taxes was $2,560, and the prorated insurance fee was $900

Figure 16.1

Lease Type: ____________________ Lease Type: ____________________ Lease Type: ____________________

Rent: ____________________ Rent: ____________________ Rent: ____________________

Answer Key

MATCHING

1. lease
2. reversionary right
3. tenancy for years
4. periodic tenancy
5. tenancy at will
6. tenancy at sufferance
7. sublease
8. option
9. actual eviction
10. constructive eviction

TRUE OR FALSE

1. False In a lease agreement, the landlord is the lessor and the tenant is the lessee.
2. True
3. True
4. False Although an extension of a tenancy for years requires a new contract, the lease may be terminated prior to the expiration date only if both parties agree or if one party has breached the agreement.
5. True
6. True
7. False The covenant of quiet enjoyment is a guarantee by the landlord that the tenant is entitled to possession of the premises without interference from the landlord.
8. True
9. True
10. False Under a gross lease agreement, the landlord pays all the operating expenses of the property, while the tenant pays only a fixed rental.
11. False Ground leases are generally long-term net leases and are often recorded.
12. True
13. False To be entitled to constructive eviction, the tenant must show only that the premises have become unusable for the purpose stated in the lease due to the landlord's conscious neglect.
14. True
15. False The landlord promises possession and the tenant promises rent; that is sufficient. Security deposits are available for unpaid rent and/or damages to the property

MULTIPLE CHOICE

1. B Even though tenants pay their own utilities, the one lump sum every month to the landlord is a gross lease. In a net lease, the tenant is responsible for paying all or part of the taxes, maintenance and insurance. Percentage leases are generally used by retail establishments and are based on gross sales.
2. A The tenant typically pays a higher "rent" with a portion being applied to the subsequent purchase of the property. It differs from a sale leaseback, whereby the owner of the property wants to pull equity from the building. The owner sells the building and agrees to rent it back.
3. C The tenants have the right to possess the property to the end of their lease. The new owners will have to wait to move in.
4. D This lease will be terminated May 1, an estate for years. By definition, no notice is required. If the landlord wants notice, he or she will have to add a paragraph to override this fact.
5. D Any lease that automatically renews itself is a periodic tenancy. It will continue on until either party gives proper notice he or she wishes to make a change.

Answer Key (Continued)

6. C This is a sublease because the tenant has given up possession for some of the remaining portion of the lease. Giving up all of the remaining rights would be an assignment. In either situation, the lessee is still responsible for the rental obligation.

7. D Constructive eviction is a result of the landlord not providing essential service, i.e., the place is unsafe or impossible to live in, conditions that are not met in this situation.

8. A Typically, if a residential rental unit is destroyed, the lease is terminated. This may or may not be the situation in a commercial or industrial lease.

9. C Both leases are covered by the statute of frauds in that one is a year in length and the other will be performed more than a year later.

10. D This is an example of an estate for years. If the tenant does not pay rent, it will be a tenancy at sufferance. If the tenant pays rent and the landlord accepts it, it will be a periodic tenancy, which could be changed into an estate for years if they enter into yet another year-long lease.

11. B The landlord is suffering because he or she does not have possession and no rent.

12. B Both the Fair Housing Laws and the Americans with Disabilities Act use the concept of "reasonable" when discussing modifications. The extent of the modifications noted would seem to be out of the scope of "reasonable."

13. B Many retail shopping centers utilize percentage leases. Part of the tenant's success is due to location. Landlords will help with promotional events to draw in customers knowing that the more successful the tenant, the more rent for the landlord.

14. C A ground lease is generally for a long period, sometimes fifty years. The tenant will often record the lease to serve constructive notice of their long-term interest.

15. C While rights to possession may be assigned or sublet, the obligation to pay rent may not be assigned to another party unless the landlord agrees to the plan. Release from liability is also called novation.

TYPES OF COMMERCIAL LEASES

Acrylic Acres

has a net lease, with $2,902.50 rent for the current month, calculated as follows:

($6,790 Utilities + $2,560 Taxes) x 15% =	$1,402.50
Base rent =	1,500.00
Total rent =	$2,902.50

Blue Buttons Boutique

has a gross lease, with $2,000 rent for the current month With a gross lease, no calculations are required. The tenant pays the rent, the landlord takes care of all expenses.

Custom Custards

has a percentage lease, with $2,515 rent for the current month calculated as follows:

$9,542 Gross Sales - $,4000 Forgiven Sales =	$5,542.00
$5,542.00 Qualifying Sales x 12% =	$ 665.04
Base rent =	1,850.00
Total rent =	$2,515.04

17 Property Management

Matching

Write the matching term on the appropriate line.

- management agreement
- consequential loss
- multiperil
- preventive maintenance
- life cycle costing
- risk management
- casualty
- audit
- tenant improvements
- surety bond

1. ______________ The document that creates the agency relationship between an owner and property manager
2. ______________ The process of determining both the initial and operating costs of equipment over its expected life
3. ______________ Performance of regularly scheduled activities such as painting and servicing appliances and systems
4. ______________ Major alterations to a building's interior to meet a tenant's particular needs
5. ______________ Evaluating and preparing for potential liabilities
6. ______________ An owner's protection against financial losses due to an employee's criminal acts
7. ______________ Insurance policies that offer a package of standard coverages
8. ______________ Insurance policies that provide coverage against theft, burglary and vandalism
9. ______________ Insurance that covers the results of a disaster
10. ______________ An investigation to determine the need for insurance and types of insurance required

True or False

Circle the answer

1. T F A property manager has three principal responsibilities: financial management, physical management and administrative management.
2. T F The management agreement creates a special agency relationship between an owner and the property manager.
3. T F Unlike real estate brokers' commissions, property management fees may be standardized by local associations.
4. T F Rental rates are influenced primarily by supply and demand.
5. T F If the vacancy rate in a building is high, the rent is probably too high.

True or False (Continued)

6. T F The manager of a residential building should carefully consider a prospective tenant's compatibility with existing tenants.

7. T F A high tenant turnover rate results in higher profits for the owner.

8. T F The four types of maintenance necessary to keep a property in good condition are preventive, corrective, rehabilitation and ordinary.

9. T F Corrective maintenance helps prevent problems and expenses before they arise.

10. T F Tenant improvements are major alterations to the interior of commercial or industrial property, usually performed by the tenant prior to moving in.

11. T F Under Title I of the ADA, all existing barriers must be removed from both residential and commercial properties.

12. T F The ADA requirements for construction built after 1991 are stricter than those for preexisting buildings.

13. T F The four alternative risk management techniques are transfer, control, avoid and retain.

14. T F In a commercial property, the risk of a shopper suffering a slip-and-fall injury would be covered by casualty insurance.

15. T F A building is insured for what it would cost to rebuild it in a depreciated value policy.

Multiple Choice

Circle A, B, C or D

1. A property manager's first responsibility to the owner should be to
   A. keep the building's occupancy rate at 100 percent.
   B. report all day-to-day financial and operating decisions to the owner on a regular basis.
   C. realize the highest profit possible consistent with the owner's instructions.
   D. ensure that the rental rates are below market average.

2. The property manager's relationship with the owner is most similar to that of a(n)
   A. partner in a partnership.
   B. employee in a store.
   C. stockholder in a corporation.
   D. real estate agent.

3. All of the following should be included in a written management agreement, EXCEPT
   A. list of the manager's duties and responsibilities.
   B. statement of the owner's purpose.
   C. statement identifying the manager's creditors.
   D. allocation of costs.

4. If apartment 3B rents for $750 per month and the manager receives a 12 percent commission on all new tenants, how much will the manager receive when he or she rents 3B, assuming that this commission is calculated in the usual way?
   A. $90
   B. $750
   C. $1,080
   D. $1,800

5. What would be the annual rent per square foot for a 30 x 40 foot property that rents for $2,950 per month?
   A. $1.20
   B. $2.46
   C. $24.65
   D. $29.50

6. A high vacancy rate most likely indicates
   A. rental rates are too low.
   B. the property is desirable.
   C. building management is effective and responsive.
   D. tenant dissatisfaction.

Multiple Choice (Continued)

7. Which of the following is an example of corrective maintenance?
   A. Seasonal servicing of appliances
   B. Picking up litter in common areas
   C. Repairing a hot water heater
   D. Moving a partition wall to make a larger office

8. The Americans with Disabilities Act applies to
   A. commercial and residential properties and all employers.
   B. commercial properties and employers of persons with disabilities.
   C. commercial properties and employers of at least 15 employees.
   D. new residential construction and employers of at least 15 people.

9. Under the ADA, existing barriers must be removed
   A. in all public buildings by the end of 1997.
   B. only on request from a person with a disability.
   C. when achievable in a "reasonably inexpensive manner."
   D. when removal may be accomplished in a "readily achievable manner."

10. A company was moving from one part of the city to another. During the move, a computer worth more than $750,000 was accidentally dropped into the river. Fortunately, the company was insured under several policies. The policy that would most likely cover the computer during the move from one facility to another is a
    A. consequential loss, use and occupancy policy.
    B. casualty policy.
    C. contents and personal property policy.
    D. liability policy.

Types of Maintenance

Identify each maintenance item listed below as Preventative, Corrective, Routine, or Construction. Mark the approximate location of each item on the floor plan shown in figure 17.1.

Figure 17.1

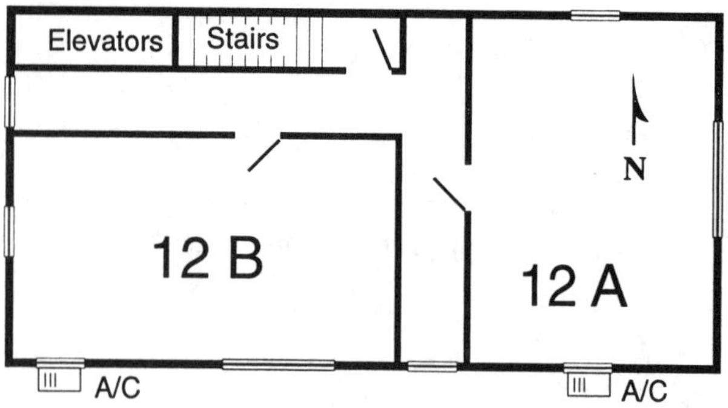

1. Paint 12th floor east-west hallway ________
____

2. Fix air conditioner in 12B: blows hot ________
____

3. Repoint exterior brick on west side ________
____

4. Replace stained carpet on stair landing ________
____

5. Repair cracked window, hallway-south ________
____

6. Annual elevator inspection and repair ________
____

7. Widen doorway in unit 12A and replace door to accommodate tenant in wheelchair ________
____

Flash Cards (Pull out page & cut with scissors)

casualty insurance	property manager
corrective maintenance	risk management
life cycle costing	surety bond
management agreement	tenant improvement
multiperil policy	rent
preventative maintenance	worker's compensation act

Property manager (agent) is hired by the owner (principal) to maintain owner's investment and ensure that the property produces income

Chapter 17

Coverage against theft, burglary, vandalism and machinery damage; health and accident insurance; often written for specific risks, i.e., theft, rather than all-inclusive

Chapter 17

Perils of any risk evaluated in terms of options: avoid, control, transfer or retain (ACTOR); often involves buying insurance to transfer risk to third party

Chapter 17

Actual repairs that keep building equipment functioning; i.e., repairing a boiler, fixing a leaky faucet, fixing an air conditioner

Chapter 17

Cover an owner against financial losses resulting from employee's criminal acts or negligence while performing assigned duties

Chapter 17

Initial and operating costs of equipment over its expected life must be measured to compare total cost of one type of equipment with that of another

Chapter 17

Alterations to building to meet commercial or industrial tenant's particular space needs; must clarify trade fixtures (tenant's personal property) vs. landlord ownership

Chapter 17

Document setting up an agency relationship between owner and property manager who is general agent establishing the rights and duties of each party

Chapter 17

Fixed, periodic payment made by tenant to owner for possession and use, usually by prior agreement of the parties

Chapter 17

Insurance package for apartment, commercial buildings; standard fire, hazard, public liability and casualty, require special coverage for earthquakes and floods

Chapter 17

Covers claims for medical or hospital payment for injuries sustained by building employees hurt in the course of employment

Chapter 17

Regularly scheduled maintenance to prevent costly breakdowns; i.e., painting and seasonal servicing of appliances and systems

Chapter 17

Answer Key

MATCHING

1. management agreement
2. life cycle costing
3. preventive maintenance
4. tenant improvements
5. risk management
6. surety bond
7. multiperil
8. casualty
9. consequential loss
10. audit

TRUE OR FALSE

1. True
2. False The management agreement creates a general agency relationship between an owner and the property manager.
3. False Like real estate brokers' commissions, property management fees may not be standardized by local associations, but must be negotiated between the parties.
4. True
5. False If the vacancy rate in a building is high, the rent is not necessarily too high.
6. False The manager of a commercial building should carefully consider a prospective tenant's compatibility with existing tenants, i.e., traffic counts, noise, etc.
7. False A high tenant turnover rate results in lower profits for the owner.
8. False The four types of maintenance necessary to keep a property in good condition are preventive, corrective, construction and routine.
9. False Preventive maintenance helps prevent problems and expenses before they arise.
10. False Tenant improvements are major alterations to the interior of commercial or industrial property, usually performed by the property manager.
11. False Under Title III of the ADA, existing barriers must be removed from commercial properties when this can be accomplished in a readily achievable manner.
12. True
13. True
14. False In a commercial property, insurance against the risk of a shopper suffering a slip-and-fall injury would be covered by liability insurance.
15. False A building is insured for what it would cost to rebuild it in a current replacement cost policy.

MULTIPLE CHOICE

1. C Keeping the building full could easily be achieved by offering below-market rates; not wise. The manager has been hired to spare the owner of day-to-day management, C is most complete.
2. D A property manager is hired as a general agent with broad authority and for a long time. A and C are quasi-owners, and an employee rarely has much authority.
3. C A management agreement sets up owner and manager responsibilities, who pays for what, all in keeping with the owner's purpose.
4. A \$750 x 12 % = \$90
5. D 30 x 40 = 1,200 square feet \$2,950 x 12 = \$35,400 ÷ 1,200 = \$29.50
6. D People will rent if the rates are attractively too low, if the building is desirable, and when the manager is responsive.

Answer Key (Continued)

7. C Corrective maintenance is fixing what is broken. Seasonal servicing is preventive; picking up litter is routine; moving a partition wall is construction.

8. C There are some exemptions for small companies.

9. D The key is "readily achievable manner."

10. C Contents and personal property insurance covers building contents and personal property during periods when they are not actually located on the business premises. Consequential loss is also known as loss or rent or business interruptions; casualty covers theft, vandalism, machinery damage; liability covers injuries sustained on the premises.

TYPES OF MAINTENANCE

1. preventive or routine
2. corrective
3. preventive
4. corrective
5. corrective
6. preventive
7. construction

Figure 17.1

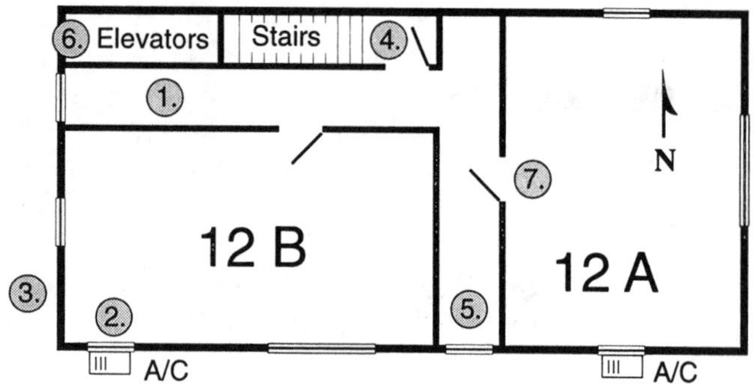

Real Estate Appraisal

18

Matching (A)

Write the matching term on the appropriate line.

- anticipation
- appraisal
- appraiser
- assemblage
- change
- conformity
- contribution
- highest and best use
- income approach
- market value

1. ________________ An estimate or opinion of value, based on supportable evidence and approved methods
2. ________________ An independent professional who is trained to provide an unbiased estimate of value
3. ________________ An estimate of value based on the present worth to the rights of future income
4. ________________ The most probable price that a property should bring in a fair sale
5. ________________ The principle that value is created by the expectation that certain events will occur in the future
6. ________________ The principle that no physical or economic condition remains constant
7. ________________ The principle that value is created when a property is in harmony with its surroundings
8. ________________ The principle that the value of any part of a property is measured by its effect on the value of the whole property
9. ________________ The most profitable single use to which property may be put
10. ________________ The process of merging two separately owned lots under one owner

Circle the answer True or False

1. T F Title XI of FIRREA requires that all residential property be appraised by a federally licensed or certified appraiser.
2. T F A competitive market analysis should never be represented as an appraisal.
3. T F The market value of a property is what it actually sells for in an open market transaction.
4. T F Cost and market value are the same.
5. T F The value of a property may be affected by events that have not actually occurred.
6. T F The law of diminishing returns applies when, no matter how much money is spent on a property, its value will not keep pace with the expenditures.

True or False (Continued)

7. T F According to the economic principle of plottage, combining two adjacent lots into a larger one will produce a higher total land value than the sum of the value of the two sites if owned separately.

8. T F The economic principle of contribution holds that the maximum value of a property tends to be set by the cost of purchasing a similarly desirable property.

9. T F In the sales comparison approach to value, a feature that is present in the subject property but not present in a comparable property is subtracted from the sale price of the comparable.

10. T F The square-foot method and the unit-in-place method are both characteristics of the cost approach to value.

11. T F Depreciation may be curable or incurable, depending on whether the expense required contributes to the property's value.

12. T F External obsolescence is always incurable.

13. T F The income approach to value is based on the future value of the rights to present income.

14. T F A GRM or GIM is often used as a substitute for an income capitalization analysis.

15. T F Reconciliation involves averaging the results derived from the three approaches to value.

Multiple Choice

Circle A, B, C or D

1. A property is listed for sale at $235,000. A buyer's offer of $220,000 is rejected by the seller. Six months later, the seller reduces the price to $205,000. Another buyer offers $210,000 and the seller accepts. The property is subsequently appraised at $215,000. Which of these figures accurately represents the property's market value?
   A. $210,000 C. $225,000
   B. $215,000 D. $235,000

2. Which appraisal approach would be best to appraise a 25-year old house in a 30-year old neighborhood?
   A. Sales comparison C. Cost approach
   B. Income approach D. GRM

3. When appraising a brand new home, in which no one has ever lived, the appraiser will lean towards the
   A. sales comparison approach.
   B. income approach.
   C. cost approach.
   D. GRM.

4. All of the following properties would have to be appraised by a state licensed or certified appraiser as required by FIRREA, assuming that all of the transactions are federally related, EXCEPT
   A. commercial property valued at $2.5 million.
   B. condominium unit with a sales price of $67,850.
   C. residential property valued at $262,500.
   D. commercial property valued over $1 million in a refinance.

5. What is the role of an appraiser?
   A. Ignore value
   B. Average values
   C. Determine value
   D. Estimate value

6. The principle that maximum value is realized when land use is in harmony with surrounding standards is
   A. contribution.
   B. conformity.
   C. highest and best use.
   D. competition.

Flash Cards (Pull out page & cut with scissors)

anticipation	highest and best use
assemblage	market value
conformity	progression, regression
cost approach	reproduction cost
economic life	square-foot method
functional obsolescence	supply and demand

Possible use of a property that would produce the greatest net income and thereby develop the highest value; making an office building where a parking lot once stood

Chapter 18

Appraisal principle that holds that value can increase or decrease based on the expectation that some future event may or may not occur

Chapter 18

Most probable price a property would bring in an arm's length transaction under normal market conditions on the open market; market price is what is actually paid

Chapter 18

Combining of two or more adjoining lots into one larger tract to increase their total value

Chapter 18

Value of properties near a better property see their values rise; the opposite is regression; a rundown property will negatively affect neighboring properties

Chapter 18

Appraisal principle that holds that the greater the similarity among properties in an area, the better they will hold their value

Chapter 18

Construction cost at current prices of an exact duplicate of the subject property; i.e., using slate shingles on the roof instead of equally effective fiberglass shingles

Chapter 18

Process of estimating property value by adding to estimated land value the appraiser's estimate of the cost of the building new, less depreciation

Chapter 18

Appraisal method of estimating building costs: multiplying number of square feet in the improvement by cost per square foot of recently constructed similar properties

Chapter 18

Number of years during which an improvement will add value to the land

Chapter 18

Interrelationship of availability of properties and desire for those properties; real estate is affected by marketplace just like most commodities

Chapter 18

Loss of value to an improvement to real estate because of functional problems, often caused by changing tastes or poor design

Chapter 18

Flash Cards (Pull out page & cut with scissors)

appraisal, appraiser	income approach
capitalization rate	physical deterioration
contribution	plottage
depreciation	replacement cost
external obsolescence	sales comparison approach
gross rent multiplier	substitution

Process of estimating value of an income-producing property through capitalization of annual net income expected from property during remaining useful life

Chapter 18

Process of estimating property value; done by the appraiser; refers also to report setting forth the process and conclusion of value

Chapter 18

Reduction in property value resulting from a decline in physical condition; i.e., wear and tear or action of the elements

Chapter 18

Rate of return a property will produce on the owner's investment

Chapter 18

Increase in value or utility resulting from the consolidation (assemblage) of two or more adjoining lots into one larger lot

Chapter 18

Appraisal principle: value of any component of a property is measured by its effect on value as a whole; cost of new swimming pool may not be returned at sale

Chapter 18

Construction cost at current prices of a property that is not exact duplicate but serves the same purpose as the original; i.e., fiberglass shingles instead of the more expensive slate

Chapter 18

In appraising, loss of value in property due to any cause; including physical deterioration, functional obsolescence and external obsolescence

Chapter 18

Process of estimating value of property by examining and comparing actual sales of comparable properties

Chapter 18

Also known as external depreciation, is a reduction in property's value caused by outside factors (those that are off the property and outside the owner's control)

Chapter 18

Appraisal principle that maximum value of property tends to be set by cost of buying an equally desirable and valuable substitute property; basis of sales comparison approach

Chapter 18

Figure used as a multiplier of the gross monthly income of a property to produce an estimate of property's value; a correlation between rent paid and ultimate sale price

Chapter 18

Multiple Choice (Continued)

7. K plans to build a large house in a neighborhood of smaller homes, so K purchases three neighboring lots from their three owners. What is the term for K's activity?
   A. Substitution
   B. Plottage
   C. Progression
   D. Assemblage

8. L buys a small house in a desirable neighborhood of large Victorian homes and pays $190,000. L's friend M buys a nearly identical house in a neighborhood of similar homes and pays $100,000. What economic principle best describes the reason why L paid more than M?
   A. Plottage
   B. Substitution
   C. Regression
   D. Progression

9. If Blandacre were vacant, undeveloped land it would be worth about $40,000. To build Blandacre Manor and its various improvements today would cost approximately $200,000. As it currently exists, Blandacre Manor's physical deterioration equals about $30,000. If an appraiser were to apply the cost approach, what would be Blandacre's value?
   A. $130,000
   B. $210,000
   C. $220,000
   D. $240,000

10. In which approach to value are the square-foot method, the unit-in-place method and the quantity-survey method used?
    A. Sales comparison approach
    B. Cost approach
    C. Income approach
    D. Reconciliation approach

11. The Ghastlie Theatre Building is considered a premier example of external ornamentation. Carved marble gargoyles and granite baskets of glazed terra cotta fruit decorate the entire front of the building. Unfortunately, increased automobile traffic in the downtown area has resulted in air pollution that has dissolved much of the intricate detail work. The cost of restoring the front of the building is roughly five times the building's present value. These facts describe which of the following?
    A. Curable external obsolescence
    B. Incurable functional obsolescence
    C. Incurable physical deterioration
    D. Curable external deterioration

12. The land on which Crumbling Manor was built is worth $50,000. The Manor was constructed in 1975 at a cost of $265,000 and is expected to last 50 years. Using the straight-line method, determine how much Crumbling Manor has depreciated by 1999.
    A. $28,600
    B. $96,600
    C. $127,200
    D. $145,200

13. Which of the following reports would a salesperson most likely research and deliver to a prospective seller?
    A. Competitive market analysis
    B. Appraisal
    C. Letter of intent
    D. Cost benefit analysis

14. What is the GRM for a three-unit apartment building with a selling price of $362,500 if the monthly rent for each apartment is $900?
    A. 1.087
    B. 108.8
    C. 134.3
    D. 402.8

15. Which of the following approaches is given the greatest weight in reconciling the appraised value of a two-bedroom, owner-occupied home?
    A. Income approach
    B. Sales comparison approach
    C. Cost approach
    D. Market value approach

16. The very old historical house has a leaking slate roof. The Historical Society demands that the new roof be made of slate. This is an example of
    A. reproduction.
    B. replacement.
    C. regression.
    D. substitution.

17. The house has been on the market for several months because most buyers do not want to walk through the master bedroom to reach another bedroom in the back. This floor plan is an example of
    A. regression.
    B. economic obsolescence.
    C. functional obsolescence
    D. physical deterioration.

Multiple Choice (Continued)

18. The owner is considering remodeling his kitchen. He could spend a fair amount of money. Before he starts, he should consider the concept of
    - A. change.
    - B. competition with the neighbors.
    - C. conformity within the neighbor.
    - D. contribution.

19. All of the following formulas are correct, EXCEPT
    - A. Income ÷ Value = Rate.
    - B. Income ÷ Rate = Value.
    - C. Value ÷ Rate = Income.
    - D. Value x Rate = Income.

20. A beautiful old mansion sits on the corner of a busy intersection. Two of the corners are occupied by gas stations, and directly across from the mansion is a fast food place. The mansion owners have been told that the property would be worth more if the lot were vacant. This is an example of
    - A. progression.
    - B. highest and best use.
    - C. regression.
    - D. conservation.

Matching (B)

Write the matching term on the appropriate line.

- cost approach
- depreciation
- economic life
- sales comparison
- regression
- replacement cost
- reproduction cost
- plottage
- supply and demand
- substitution

1. ______________ The principle that merging or consolidating adjacent lots into a single one will produce a higher total value than the sum of the two sites valued separately
2. ______________ The principle that the worth of a better-quality property is adversely affected by the presence of a lesser-quality property
3. ______________ The principle that the maximum value of a property tends to be set by how much it would cost to purchase an equally desirable property
4. ______________ The economic principle that the value of a property depends on the number of similar properties available in the marketplace
5. ______________ The approach that estimates value by comparing the subject property with recently sold similar properties
6. ______________ An estimate of value by determining the value of the land as if it were vacant, adding the current cost of constructing improvements and deducting accrued depreciation
7. ______________ The cost of constructing an exact duplicate of the subject property at current prices
8. ______________ The current price of constructing a property similar to the subject property
9. ______________ A loss in value due to any cause
10. ______________ The period during which a property is expected to remain useful for its original intended purpose

Pennytree Lane Appraisals

Complete the appraisal problems below based on the five homes on the 1200 block of Pennytree Lane depicted in Figure 18.1

Figure 18.1

1. 1230 Pennytree Lane was just sold. Which house is the best comparable property? __________________
2. The principle of regression is best illustrated by which properties? __________________
3. The principle of progression is best illustrated by which properties? __________________
4. Pennytree Lane is near an increasingly fashionable and upscale part of town. Incomes in the area are rising rapidly. If 1236 is a newly constructed home, it is an example of which principle of value? __________________
5. When 1232 added a garage, what likely happened to the values of 1230 and 1234? __________________
6. House number 1236 violates which principle of value? __________________
7. When 1234 added a satellite dish, which principle to value describes its effect? __________________

Answer Key

MATCHING (A)

1. appraisal
2. appraiser
3. income approach
4. market value
5. anticipation
6. change
7. conformity
8. contribution
9. highest and best use
10. assemblage

TRUE OR FALSE

1. False Title XI of FIRREA requires that all residential property valued at $250,000 or more in a federally related transaction be appraised by a state licensed or certified appraiser.
2. True

Answer Key (True or False - Continued)

3. False The market price of a property is what it actually sells for in an open market transaction.

4. False Cost and market value may be, but are not necessarily, the same.

5. True

6. True

7. True

8. False The economic principle of substitution holds that the maximum value of a property tends to be set by the cost of purchasing a similarly desirable property.

9. False In the sales approach to value, a feature that is present in the subject property but not present in a comparable property is added to the sales price of the comparable.

10. True

11. True

12. True

13. False The income approach to value is based on the present value of the rights to future income.

14. True

15. False Reconciliation involves a detailed and professional analysis and application of the three approaches to value, not simply an average of the different values.

MULTIPLE CHOICE

1. A The value has been set by the agreement between the buyer and the seller.

2. A The most appropriate method to appraise an older home in an established neighborhood is the sales comparison approach.

3. C A newly constructed house may be appraised using the cost approach and omitting depreciation.

4. B Appraisals of residential property valued at \$250,000 or less and commercial property valued at \$1 million or less in federally related transactions are exempt and need not be performed by licensed or certified appaisers.

5. D An appraiser estimates value.

6. B Contribution is the principle that evaluates the cost of adding an improvement against the value of the property as a whole. Competition is the interaction of supply and demand, while highest and best use is the most profitable single use to which the property may be used.

7. D The process of merging two separately owned lots under one owner is called assemblage. Plottage holds that merging these lots together into a single larger one produces a great total land value than the sum of the individual lots valued separately.

8. D L's house benefits from being a smaller one alongside larger, most prestigious ones, i.e., progression. M's house is appropriately valued for its neighborhood.

9. B The cost approach subtracts the depreciation from the cost of today's improvements and then adds on the value of the land as if it were vacant: \$200,000 - \$30,000 + \$40,000 = \$210,000

10. B Sales approach compares values of comparable properties; income approach places a value on acquiring future income.

11. C Air pollution has irreparably destroyed the old design. This is an example of incurable, physical deterioration.

12. C The value of the land is not relevant to this problem. The cost of the building is divided by the number of years of its useful life and multiplied to determine the depreciation after 24 years: \$265,000 ÷ 50 = \$5,300 x 24 = \$127,200

13. A A real estate salesperson often prepares a competitive market analysis (CMA), a comparison of the prices of recently sold homes that are similar to a listing seller's home in terms of location, style and amenities. This helps the owner set an appropriate asking price for his or her property.

14. C Value divided by gross rent equals gross rent multiplier: \$362,500 ÷ \$2,700 = 134.3

Answer Key (Multiple Choice - Continued)

15. B Most owner-occupied residences are best appraised by comparing them to similar properties, i.e., sales comparison approach.

16. A Construction cost at current prices of an exact duplicate of the subject improvement is called reproduction; i.e., slate for slate. The roof could be replaced with a modern material at a lower cost and be just as effective at keeping the rain out of the house.

17. C There is nothing physically wrong with the house, but the design is outdated, i.e., functionally obsolescent. Perhaps buyers would be more interested if the room were changed to an office use.

18. D Before embarking on a major remodeling job, the owner should consider its overall contribution to the value of the property, especially along side his neighbors. Sometimes, the improvement does not add value equal to its cost.

19. C C should read value x rate = income

20. B The single most profitable use for this property is not a residential mansion; more likely, it would be better suited to another gas station or convenience store.

MATCHING (B)

1. plottage
2. regression
3. substitution
4. supply and demand
5. sales comparison
6. cost approach
7. reproduction cost
8. replacement cost
9. depreciation
10. economic life

PENNYTREE LANE APPRAISALS

1. 1234
2. 1238 lowers the value of 1236 and 1234
3. 1236 raises the value of 1234 and 1238
4. anticipation
5. values declined
6. conformity
7. contribution

19 Land-Use Controls and Property Development

Matching (A)

Write the matching term on the appropriate line.

- buffer zones
- bulk zoning
- comprehensive plan
- conditional-use permit
- enabling acts
- master plan
- nonconforming use
- taking
- variance
- zoning ordinances

1. ______________ The device by which local governments establish development goals
2. ______________ Another term for a community's proposed framework for controlling growth and development
3. ______________ Local laws that implement a comprehensive plan and regulate the control of land and structures within districts
4. ______________ The legal means by which states confer zoning powers on local governments
5. ______________ Areas such as parks used to screen residential from nonresidential areas
6. ______________ A special type of zoning used to control density by imposing restrictions such as setbacks or limiting new construction
7. ______________ The seizure of land through the government's power of eminent domain or condemnation
8. ______________ A lot or improvement that is not in harmony with current zoning because it existed prior to the enactment or amendment of the zoning
9. ______________ The device by which a day-care center might be permitted to operate in a residential neighborhood
10. ______________ The device by which a landowner may use his or her property in a manner that is otherwise strictly prohibited by the existing zoning ordinances

Circle the answer — *True or False*

1. T F Zoning ordinances create the broad, general framework for a community; the comprehensive plan defines the details and implements the ordinances.

2. T F Bulk zoning is used to ensure that certain types of uses are incorporated into developments.

Flash Cards (Pull out page & cut with scissors)

buffer zone	Interstate Land Sales Full Disclosure Act
building code	nonconforming use
clustering	subdivider
conditional-use permit	taking
deed restriction	variance
developer	zoning ordinance

Federal law that regulates the sale of certain real estate in interstate commerce

Chapter 19

Strip of land separating one type of use from another; i.e., a park or running trails between the commercial buildings and the residential neighborhood

Chapter 19

Use of property that is permitted to continue after a zoning ordinance prohibiting it has been established for the area

Chapter 19

Ordinance that specifies minimum standards of construction for buildings to protect public safety and health

Chapter 19

One who buys undeveloped land, divides it into smaller, usable lots and sells the lots to potential users

Chapter 19

Grouping of home sites within a subdivision on smaller lots than normal, with the remaining land used as common areas

Chapter 19

From the "takings" clause of the 5th Amendment to U.S. Constitution, "nor shall public property be taken for public use, without just compensation"

Chapter 19

Written governmental permission allowing the use inconsistent with the zoning, but necessary for the public good; i.e., emergency medical facility in residential area

Chapter 19

Permission obtained from zoning authorities to build a structure or conduct a use that is expressly prohibited by current zoning laws; an exception from zoning ordinances

Chapter 19

Clause in deed limiting future use of property; may limit density of buildings, dictate types of structures or even prevent buildings from being used for a specific purpose

Chapter 19

An exercise of police power by a municipality to regulate and control the character and use of property

Chapter 19

Person who attempts to put land to its most profitable use through the construction of improvements

Chapter 19

True or False *(Continued)*

3. T F Property owners are protected against the unreasonable or arbitrary taking of their land by the seizure clause of the Fifteenth Amendment to the United States Constitution.

4. T F The government's payment to a landowner for seizure of his or her property is referred to as "just compensation."

5. T F A conditional use permit allows a landowner to use his or her property in a manner that is otherwise strictly prohibited by the existing zoning.

6. T F Zoning permits are usually required before building permits can be issued.

7. T F A subdivider is a person who buys undeveloped acreage and divides it into smaller lots for sale to individuals or developers.

8. T F A detailed map that illustrates the geographic boundaries of individual lots is called a plan.

9. T F Zoning is a state and local issue; there is no national zoning ordinance.

10. T F The average number of units per acre in a development is referred to as the development's gross density.

11. T F A restrictive covenant is considered a reasonable, legal restraint if it protects property values or restricts the free transfer of property.

12. T F The Interstate Land Sales Full Disclosure Act requires developers of any property to file a disclosure statement with HUD.

13. T F Communities develop comprehensive plans to control growth and development

14. T F Clustering housing units can dramatically increase the amount of open and recreational space within a development

15. T F Through power conferred by state enabling acts, local governments exercise public controls based on the state's obligation to protect public health, safety and welfare

Multiple Choice

Circle A, B, C or D

1. A restrictive covenant is included in the deeds for all properties in the Liberty Cove subdivision, which was built in 1962. The covenant bans "all outdoor structures designed for the storage of equipment or as habitations for any animals for 32 years from the date recorded on the original plat of subdivision." In 1997, a resident built a tool shed and a doghouse. Do the neighbors have any recourse?
   - A. Yes; they can go to court and sue for monetary damages for violating the covenant.
   - B. Yes; they can go to court and be awarded injunctive relief.
   - C. No; the restrictive covenant is no longer operative unless the property owners of Liberty Cove have agreed to its extension.
   - D. No; restrictive covenants such as this are usually considered to be unenforceable restrictions on the free transfer of property.

2. A state delegates zoning powers to a municipality through
   - A. its police power.
   - B. eminent domain.
   - C. a comprehensive plan.
   - D. an enabling act.

3. All of the following would be included in a zoning ordinance, EXCEPT
   - A. permissible height and style of new construction.
   - B. objectives for future development of the area.
   - C. style and appearance of structures.
   - D. the maximum allowable ratio of land area to structural area.

Multiple Choice (Continued)

4. Which of the following protects a property owner against being deprived of his or her property by the government without just compensation?
   A. The Preamble to the U.S. Constitution
   B. The "takings clause" of the Fifth Amendment to the U.S. Constitution
   C. The "due process" clause of the Fourteenth Amendment to the U.S. Constitution
   D. The "compensation clause" of Article VII of the Bill of Rights

5. The city of Onion Lake has passed a new zoning ordinance that prohibits all commercial structures over 30 feet high. R wants to build an office building that will be 45 feet high. Under these facts, which of the following statements is true?
   A. R must apply for a nonconforming use permit.
   B. R must apply for a zoning permit.
   C. R must apply for a conditional-use permit.
   D. R must apply for a variance.

6. L would like to operate a plant-sitting business in his home, but he lives in an area zoned for residential use only. What should L do?
   A. Request that the zoning board declare his home to be a nonconforming use
   B. Ask a court to grant an injunction against the zoning board
   C. Seek a conditional-use permit from the zoning board
   D. Apply to the zoning board for a variance

7. N goes all over the country buying large tracts of vacant land, splitting them into smaller parcels and building identical communities of single-family ranch-style homes surrounding a central shopping center. N sells the homes to residents and leases space in the shopping center to merchants. N is a
   A. developer.
   B. subdivider.
   C. developer and subdivider.
   D. assembler.

8. Which of the following best defines density zoning?
   A. The mandatory use of clustering
   B. The average number of units in a development
   C. A restriction on the average number of houses per acre
   D. A restriction on the average number of acres per parcel

9. Large lots, wide streets and uniformity are characteristic of
   A. clustering.
   B. the curvilinear system.
   C. the gridiron pattern.
   D. aesthetic zoning ordinances.

10. All of the following are common characteristics of a constitutionally valid zoning ordinance, EXCEPT
    A. clear and specific provisions.
    B. anticipation of future housing needs.
    C. nondiscriminatory effect.
    D. equal application.

11. P owns Heron's Nest, a 2,000-acre tract of undeveloped woodland surrounding a scenic lake in the state of North Virginia. P has divided the tract into 106 individual lots, ranging in size from 15 to 100 acres. P has hired several telemarketers to sell the lots to residents of North Virginia and the three states with which it shares a common border. Based on these facts, which of the following statements is true?
    A. P must file a disclosure statement with HUD under the Interstate Land Sales Full Disclosure Act.
    B. Because P's project is not fraudulent, it is exempt from the requirements of the Interstate Land Sales Full Disclosure Act.
    C. The Heron's Nest project is exempt from the Interstate Land Sales Full Disclosure Act because of the lot size exemption, but it must comply with any state subdivided land sales laws.
    D. P's project is exempt from the Interstate Land Sales Full Disclosure Act because it is not being marketed outside a contiguous multistate region, although it must comply with the subdivided land sales laws of each of the states in which it is actively marketed.

12. Zoning ordinances affect all of the following EXCEPT
    A. lot sizes.
    B. building heights
    C. style and appearance of buildings.
    D. racial composition of neighborhood.

Multiple Choice (Continued)

13. The developer has included a playground and running trails between the commercial properties facing the busy street and the houses further back in the subdivision. The recreational area is considered
    A. aesthetic zoning.
    B. a buffer zone.
    C. a taking.
    D. nonconforming use.

14. When the area was rezoned as residential, a tavern was grandfathered in and allowed to continue business. This is an example of
    A. a variance.
    B. nonconforming use.
    C. conditional-use permit.
    D. an amendment.

15. A new structure has been completed to the satisfaction of the inspecting city engineer. What documentation must be issued before anyone can move in?
    A. Appraisal report
    B. Certificate of occupancy
    C. Certificate of reasonable value
    D. Conditional-use permit

Matching (B)

Write the matching term on the appropriate line.

- building codes
- Interstate Land Sales Full Disclosure Act
- clustering
- density zoning
- developer
- subdivider
- building permit
- plat
- police power
- restrictive covenants

1. ______________ The device by which municipal officials are alerted to new construction and alterations
2. ______________ A person who buys undeveloped acreage and divides it into smaller lots for sale to others
3. ______________ An individual who constructs improvements and sells them
4. ______________ A detailed map that illustrates the geographic boundaries of individual lots
5. ______________ Ordinances that restrict the average maximum number of houses per acre
6. ______________ Standards for building style, setbacks and use that are included in a deed for property in a subdivision
7. ______________ Ordinances that specify construction and safety standards for construction
8. ______________ Grouping home sites on lots smaller than normal and designating the remaining land as common areas
9. ______________ Act that requires developers to file statements with HUD before they can be marketed interstate
10. ______________ State's authority to make rules needed to protect the public health, safety and welfare

Zoning in Metroville

Answer the following questions based on Metroville's zoning map depicted below.

Figure 19.1

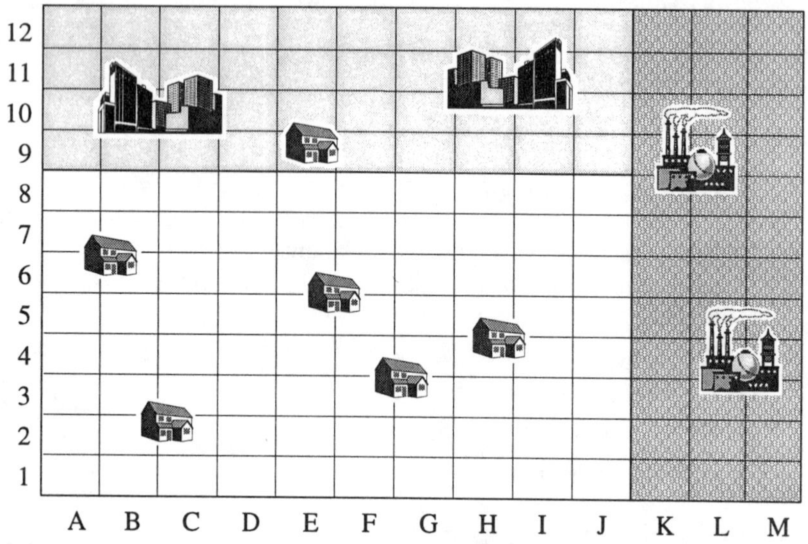

1. M owns a piece of property that includes areas J-8, J-9 and K-8. How can M use this property?

2. What would be necessary before Kiddie Kare, Inc., could legally acquire land and operate a day care center in area D5?

3. Where would it be most beneficial for Metroville to locate a new park as a buffer zone?

4. If Metroville rezones the area bounded by K-9, K-12, M-12 and M-9 as commercial, what issue might be raised for a factory owner located in the affected area?

5. The house at E-9 was built prior to Metroville's zoning ordinance. How would you describe it? Through what process is it permitted to continue being a residence?

6. Metroville has asked you where they should locate a new "retail and professional services zone," which will take up to 6 square units on the map. Where would you locate this new zone? Why?

Answer Key

MATCHING (A)

1. comprehensive plan
2. master plan
3. zoning ordinances
4. enabling acts
5. buffer zones
6. bulk zoning
7. taking
8. nonconforming use
9. conditional-use permit
10. variance

TRUE OR FALSE

1. False A comprehensive plan creates the broad, general framework for a community; zoning ordinances define the details and implement the plan.
2. False Incentive zoning is used to ensure that certain types of uses are incorporated into developments.
3. False Property owners are protected against the unreasonable or arbitrary taking of their land by the takings clause of the First Amendment to the United States Constitution.
4. True
5. False A variance allows a landowner to use his or her property in a manner that is otherwise strictly prohibited by the existing zoning.

Answer Key (Multiple Choice - Continued)

6. True
7. True
8. False A detailed map that illustrates the geographic boundaries of individual lots is called a plat.
9. True
10. True
11. False A restrictive covenant is considered a reasonable, legal restraint if it protects property values and does not restrict the free transfer of property.
12. False The Interstate Land Sales Full Disclosure Act requires developers of any unimproved property offered in interstate commerce by telephone or through the mail to file a disclosure statement with HUD.
13. True
14. True
15. True

MULTIPLE CHOICE

1. C If the neighbors were concerned, they needed to rally support and gain consent to an extension of the restrictive covenant.
2. D Enabling acts permit the state to delegate authority to local officials to enact rules to protect the public's health and safety. This police power includes creating a comprehensive plan and acquiring private property for public use through the right of eminent domain.
3. B A, C, and D all might be included in a zoning ordinance; B might be found in a comprehensive plan.
4. B The Preamble to the U.S. Constitution provides for promotion of the general welfare, but the 14th Amendment prevents states from depriving "any person of life, liberty, or property, without due process of law."
5. D Since R's building does not yet exist, it does not qualify for nonconforming use; a conditional-use permit is used for a special use that meets certain standards. A variance, if granted, will permit the landowner to use his or her property in a manner that is strictly prohibited by the existing zoning.
6. C A conditional-use permit might be granted in this situation since the intended use would not greatly impact the residential nature of the neighborhood.
7. C Subdividers buy undeveloped acreage, divide it into smaller lots. A developer improves the land, constructs homes or other buildings and sells them. Developing is usually more extensive than subdividing.
8. C Density zoning ordinances restrict the average maximum number of houses per acre that may be built within a particular subdivision. Sometimes a developer will "cluster" building lots to achieve an open effect.
9. C The gridiron pattern evolved out of the government rectangular survey system. It provides for little open space and many lots may front on busy streets, but it is easy to navigate. The curvilinear system develops smaller secondary and cul-de-sac streets, avoids the uniformity of the gridiron pattern but often lacks service alleys.
10. B Zoning ordinances cannot be static; they must remain flexible to meet the changing needs of society. The comprehensive plan would seek to anticipate future housing needs.
11. A P must file the disclosure statement: it is being marketed over state lines, is more than 25 lots and on more than 20 acres.
12. D Zoning may not discuss the racial composition of the neighborhood.
13. B A buffer zone is a strip of land usually used as a park separating land dedicated to one use (commercial) from land dedicated to another use (residential).

Answer Key (Multiple Choice - Continued)

14. B Since the tavern had been there legally before the zoning ordinance, it is permitted to continue usually until its use changes or the building is destroyed.

15. B Once the completed building has been inspected and found satisfactory, the municipal inspector issues a certificate of occupancy or occupancy permit.

MATCHING (B)

1. building permit
2. subdivider
3. developer
4. plat
5. density zoning
6. restrictive covenants
7. building codes
8. clustering
9. Interstate Land Sales Full Disclosure Act
10. police power

METROVILLE ZONING (FIGURE 19.1)

1. J-9 is in the commercial zone; J-8 may be used for residential development; K8 is limited to industrial use.

2. conditional use permit

3. J-1 through J-8 (a park would serve the residential neighborhoods and provide a buffer between the residential and industrial zones).

4. The rezoning could be a takings issue if the value of the property is decreased.

5. The house is a nonconforming use. It was most likely grandfathered in.

6. One possible location would be the square bounded by J-7, G-7, G-9 and J-9: it would provide retail services near the residential neighborhood, professional services near the commercial zone, and would not be disruptive to the industrial zone. Other possibilities include A-8 through F-8, or six units between J-1 and J-8 as a buffer. It would probably not be wise to place the new zone in the center of the residential area (due to traffic and noise), or in the industrial zone (it could present hazards to shoppers).

Fair Housing and Ethical Practices

20

Matching

Write the matching term on the appropriate line.

- familial status
- Equal Credit Opportunity Act
- Civil Rights Act of 1968
- handicap
- blockbusting
- Fair Housing Act
- ADA
- HUD
- steering
- Jones v. Mayer

1. ______________ A law that prohibits discrimination in housing based on race, color, religion and national origin
2. ______________ The Civil Rights Act of 1968, the Housing and Community Development Act of 1974 and the Fair Housing Amendments Act of 1988, collectively
3. ______________ The agency that administers the federal fair housing laws
4. ______________ The presence of one or more persons who are under the age of 18, living with a parent or adult guardian
5. ______________ A physical or mental impairment
6. ______________ A U.S. Supreme Court decision that prohibits all racial discrimination in housing
7. ______________ A law that prohibits discrimination against protected classes in evaluating loan applicants
8. ______________ A law that requires accessibility to employment, goods and services for individuals with disabilities
9. ______________ Encouraging the sale or renting of property by claiming a protected class of people are moving into the area
10. ______________ Encouraging home seekers to limit their search to particular neighborhoods based on noneconomic factors such as race or religion

True or False

Circle the answer

1. T F The purpose of the civil rights laws that affect the real estate industry is to make everyone equal.
2. T F Failing to comply with state and federal fair housing laws may subject a licensee to both fines and disciplinary action.
3. T F The Civil Rights Act of 1968 applies only to race.
4. T F Under HUD regulations, a "dwelling" is limited to single family houses, condominiums and cooperatives.

True or False (Continued)

5. T F The fair housing laws under the "disabled persons" classification protects persons with AIDS.

6. T F There are no exemptions under the federal Fair Housing Act.

7. T F The protections under the Equal Credit Opportunity Act are broader than those under the Fair Housing Act.

8. T F The ADA's specific requirements for making curb ramps, elevators and other spaces accessible for people with disabilities are contained in the "Accessibility Guidelines."

9. T F Redlining is the act of encouraging people to sell or rent their homes on the basis that the entry of members of a protected class into the neighborhood will reduce property values.

10. T F Channeling home seekers to particular neighborhoods based on noneconomic factors is an illegal practice known as steering.

11. T F There are no exceptions to HUD's rules regarding statements of preference or limitations in advertising regarding race.

12. T F While not valid considerations for the underlying real estate transaction, the following factors may be considered by an appraiser in evaluating a property: race, color, religion, national origin, sex, disability and familial status.

13. T F Any individual who believes he or she is the victim of illegal discrimination in a real estate transaction may file a complaint with HUD within three years of the alleged act.

14. T F Failure to prominently display the Equal Housing poster is prima facie evidence of discriminatory practices.

15. T F The National Association of REALTORS®, adopted a "Code of Ethics" in 1913 to establish professional standards of behavior for its member licensees.

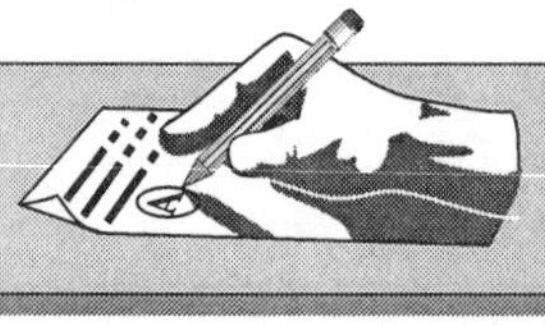

Multiple Choice

Circle A, B, C or D

1. Which of the following offer protection against discrimination in housing on the basis of race, color, religion and national origin only?
   A. Fair Housing Act
   B. Fair Housing Amendments Act of 1988
   C. Housing and Community Development Act of 1974
   D. Civil Rights Act of 1968

2. The Fair Housing Act is administered by
   A. Office of Equal Opportunity.
   B. U.S. Housing and Urban Development.
   C. Justice Department.
   D. the federal court system.

3. The Fair Housing Act prohibits discrimination on the basis of all the following factors, EXCEPT
   A. familial status.
   B. national origin.
   C. religious preference.
   D. sexual preference.

4. The Equal Credit Opportunity Act prohibits discrimination on the basis of all of the following factors, EXCEPT
   A. amount of income.
   B. source of income.
   C. marital status.
   D. age.

Flash Cards (Pull out page & cut with scissors)

Americans with Disabilities Act (ADA)	familial status
blockbusting	Jones v. Mayer
Civil Rights Act of 1866	protected classes
code of ethics	redlining
Equal Credit Opportunity Act (ECOA)	steering
Fair Housing Violation Enforcement	Title VIII of the Civil Rights Act of 1968

In fair housing, at least one person over the age of 18 having legal custody of one person under 18; includes pregnant women and foster children

Chapter 20

Protects rights of disabled individuals in employment and public accommodations; requires reasonable accommodations that enable disabled persons to work with dignity

Chapter 20

Supreme Court decision upholding Civil Rights Act of 1866; under no circumstances is anyone exempt from this law prohibiting racial discrimination

Chapter 20

Illegal practice of inducing homeowners to sell their properties by telling them that a certain people of a certain race, national origin or religion are moving into the area

Chapter 20

Any group of people designated by HUD in consideration of federal and state law; currently includes ethnic minorities, women, religious groups, handicapped and others

Chapter 20

Act that prohibits any racial discrimination in the sale or rental of housing

Chapter 20

Illegal practice of refusing to make mortgage loans or issue insurance policies in specific areas for reasons other than economic qualifications of applicants

Chapter 20

Written system of moral standards for ethical behavior that often goes beyond the letter of the law

Chapter 20

Illegal practice of channeling home seekers to particular neighborhoods based on race, religion, national origin; an illegal limitation of a purchaser's options

Chapter 20

Prohibits discrimination in lending based on race, color, religion, national origin, sex, receipt of public assistance, age and marital status

Chapter 20

Prohibits discrimination in the sale or rental of housing based on race, color, religion, national origin, sex, familial status, and handicap

Chapter 20

Unlimited punitive damages, actual damages, injunctions, fines ranging from $10,000 to $50,000

Chapter 20

Multiple Choice (Continued)

5. While real estate licensees may be ethically obligated to be aware of the requirements of the ADA, they may also have a legal obligation to comply with the act, because licensees
   A. often have clients with disabilities.
   B. frequently own their own homes.
   C. may be employers.
   D. are required to do so by the Code of Ethics.

6. W, a real estate broker, sends a bright yellow flier to all the homeowners in the Grayside Hills neighborhood. The flier contains a reprinted article from a local newspaper describing the future relocation plans of various employers in the region and the following statement, printed in bold red letters:

   "WARNING! THE FAILURE TO SELL YOUR PROPERTY WITHIN THE NEXT SIX MONTHS COULD COST YOU A BUNDLE!" At the bottom of the page was printed W's name, photo, office address and phone number. Based on these facts, which of the following statements is true?
   A. W is guilty of steering.
   B. W is guilty of blockbusting.
   C. W has committed no offense.
   D. W has violated the HUD advertising guidelines.

7. In the past six months, a local bank has been forced to foreclose on several mortgages in the mostly Asian suburb of Grand Pasture. The bank's board of directors tells the loan department to make no further loans on properties located in the suburb. Based on these facts, which of the following statements is true?
   A. The bank is guilty of redlining.
   B. The bank is in violation of the Home Mortgage Disclosure Act.
   C. The bank's action falls under the "reasonable purpose" exception to the Fair Housing Act.
   D. The bank is guilty of discrimination on the basis of race.

8. Under what conditions can someone refuse to rent to an African-American?
   A. Never
   B. If the owner is also living in one of the apartments of a small apartment building
   C. If the owner is handling the leasing without the aid of a real estate agent
   D. A small investor who is selling one of the three houses he or she owns.

9. Under the Fair Housing Acts, who is responsible for proving that the discriminatory act took place?
   A. Complainant
   B. Defendant
   C. Justice Department
   D. Administrative Law Judge (ALJ)

10. Because the region in which broker C works has homeowners of many different ethnic backgrounds, C took a three-week intensive course called "Understanding a Diverse Market." In the course, C learned about the cultural habits of people from a wide variety of countries and cultures. Now, when a prospective buyer from far-off Thabong or the highlands of Nyenska comes into C's office, C knows just which neighborhood they'd feel most comfortable living in and helps them adjust to life in the U.S. by showing them properties exclusively in areas where there are other homeowners from their homelands. Based on these facts only, C is
    A. in violation of the Civil Rights Act of 1964.
    B. committing steering, but is not guilty due to the lack of discriminatory effect.
    C. guilty of steering.
    D. not guilty of steering, because C lacks a discriminatory intent.

11. What is the statute of limitations for housing discrimination actions brought under the Civil Rights Act of 1968?
    A. 100 days
    B. 1 year
    C. 2 years
    D. The same as the statute of limitations for torts committed in the state in which the alleged discriminatory act occurred

12. Complaints of discriminatory housing practices filed with HUD will be referred to a local enforcement agency if
    A. the federal law is substantially more inclusive than the state or municipal law.
    B. HUD determines that an administrative law judge should decide the case.
    C. the state or municipal law is substantially equivalent to the federal law.
    D. the complaint involves a licensee who is the victim of a threat or act of violence because he or she has complied with the fair housing laws.

Multiple Choice (Continued)

13. The term "professional ethics" refers to
    A. the system of professional standards adopted by the National Association of REALTORS® in 1913.
    B. the requirements of the Fair Housing Act as they apply to real estate professionals.
    C. a system of moral principles, rules and standards of conduct that govern a professional's relations with consumers and colleagues.
    D. a standard of integrity and competence expected of professionals and licensees in the housing and real estate industry, established by the Department of Housing and Urban Development, symbolized by the equal housing opportunity poster.

14. All of the following classifications of people are considered protected classes EXCEPT
    A. member of Alcoholics Anonymous.
    B. blind person with seeing eye dog.
    C. AIDs patient.
    D. user of crack cocaine.

15. To raise a little grocery money, R decides to rent a spare bedroom in her single-family house to a tenant for $50 per month. When a 24-year-old man asks to see the room, R refuses, telling him that she will only rent to women over the age of 50. The prospective tenant threatens to sue for a violation of the Fair Housing Act. Should R be concerned?
    A. Yes; the amount of rent being charged is immaterial for purposes of the Fair Housing Act.
    B. Yes; while R is permitted to exclude individuals on the basis of age or sex, she cannot exclude on the basis of both.
    C. No; the rental of rooms in an owner-occupied single-family home is exempt from the Fair Housing Act.
    D. No; because there was no real estate licensee involved in this transaction, R is free to discriminate on the basis of any of the normally protected classes.

Answer Key

MATCHING ANSWERS

1. Civil Rights Act of 1866
2. Fair Housing Act
3. HUD
4. familial status
5. handicap
6. Jones v. Mayer
7. Equal Credit Opportunity Act (ECOA)
8. Americans with Disabilities Act (ADA)
9. blockbusting
10. steering

TRUE OR FALSE

1. False — The purpose of the civil rights laws that affect real estate is to create a marketplace in which all persons of similar financial means have a similar range of housing choices.
2. True
3. False — The Civil Rights Act of 1968 applies to housing discrimination based on race, color, religion and national origin.
4. False — Under HUD regulations, a "dwelling" includes single family houses, condominiums and cooperatives, mobile homes and vacant land on which any of these structures will be built.
5. True
6. False — There are no exemptions under the federal Fair Housing Act involving race, but there are some for small investors and certain organizations.
7. True
8. True

Answer Key (Continued)

9. False Blockbusting is the act of encouraging people to sell or rent their homes on the basis that the entry of members of a protected class into the neighborhood will reduce property values.
10. True
11. True
12. False Race, color, religion, national origin, sex, disability and familial status may not be considered in any formal or informal appraisal or evaluation of a property.
13. False Any individual who believes he or she is the victim of illegal discrimination in a real estate transaction may file a complaint with HUD within one year of the alleged act.
14. True
15. True

MULTIPLE CHOICE

1. D The Civil Rights Act of 1968 is the most comprehensive and has been amended several times.
2. B The U.S. Housing and Urban Development office handles fair housing complaints on the national level. Most states have enacted "substantially" similar laws, so often it is the state agency that is involved.
3. D Sexual preference is not a protected class under the federal law but has been added to many city and state fair housing laws. Protections can be added to the federal law but not deleted.
4. A The ECOA prohibits discrimination in lending for eight protected classes; however, one still has to have a source of income in order to qualify for a loan.
5. C Many real estate licensees are brokers who own an office, and the real estate office should be accessible to the public, including a handicapped person.
6. C Although perhaps in poor taste, W is distributing a published newspaper article to which anyone has access. One wonders who he will find to buy these properties after he portrays such a negative image about the neighborhood.
7. A The bank may not make a decision to make or not make loans on the basis of race, color, religion, national origin, sex, familial status, or handicap.
8. A Under the Civil Rights Act of 1866, as reinforced by the Jones v. Mayer Supreme Court decision, there are no exemptions that permit someone to discriminate in housing simply because of someone's race.
9. A One does not lose one's right to be presumed innocent until proven guilty. Certain actions, such as not prominently displaying the equal housing poster, may be considered prima facie evidence of discriminatory practices.
10. C This agent has no business placing people in neighborhoods based on their race or national origin. Buyers have the right to see homes based on their buying abilities.
11. B Persons who wish to file a complaint under Title VIII of the Civil Rights Act of 1968 must do so within one year of the alleged violation.
12. C Many states and some cities have passed Fair Housing Laws that are even more inclusive than the federal law. Protections can be added, not deleted.
13. C The National Association of REALTORS® did adopt a Code of Ethics in 1913, and it has evolved and been changed a number of times in the last 80+ years. The more complete answer, however, is letter C.
14. D Users of illegal drugs do not enjoy any protections under the Fair Housing Laws, although handicap is a protected class.
15. C The woman is exempt from the law because she will be renting a single room in her home.

21 Environmental Issues and the Real Estate Transaction

Matching

Write the matching term on the appropriate line.

- urea-formaldehyde
- electromagnetic field
- encapsulation
- capping
- landfill
- Superfund
- radon
- lead
- asbestos
- water table

1. ________________ A highly friable mineral commonly used as insulation prior to being banned in 1978
2. ________________ The process of sealing off a hazardous material without removing it
3. ________________ A material once used in paint that can cause serious brain and nervous system damage
4. ________________ A radioactive gas produced by the natural decay of other underground radioactive substances
5. ________________ An insulating foam material that can release harmful gases
6. ________________ A by-product of electrical currents that may pose a health risk
7. ________________ The natural level at which the ground is saturated
8. ________________ A site for the burial of waste
9. ________________ The process of covering a solid waste site with topsoil and plants
10. ________________ Money set aside by the Comprehensive Environmental Response, Compensation and Liability Act to pay for the clean up of uncontrolled hazardous waste sites

True or False

Circle the answer

1. T F The Environmental Protection Agency estimates that approximately 20 percent of commercial and public buildings built after 1978 contain asbestos insulation.

2. T F Asbestos removal is a relatively simple, inexpensive process that can be performed by any reasonably intelligent person.

3. T F Under the 1996 regulations published by the Environmental Protection Agency and the Department of Housing and Urban Development, owners of homes built prior to 1978 are required to test their properties for the presence of lead-based paint and must fill out a lead-based paint disclosure statement.

Flash Cards (Pull out page & cut with scissors)

asbestos	groundwater
capping	landfill
carbon monoxide	lead
Comprehensive Environmental Response, Compensation and Liability Act (CERCLA)	radon
electromagnetic field EMFs	underground storage tanks (UST)
encapsulation	urea formaldehyde foam insulation (UFFI)

Water that exists under earth's surface in tiny spaces or crevices in geological formations; if contaminated, threatens source of clean drinking water

Chapter 21

Mineral used extensively in insulation; inhaling fibers can cause sever respiratory diseases; particularly dangerous if friable, i.e., easily crumbled

Chapter 21

An enormous hole to store hazardous materials, lined to prevent leakage of waste materials; includes underground drainage pipes to monitor for leaks and leaching

Chapter 21

Process of laying two to four feet of soil over the top of a landfill site and planting grass to enhance aesthetic value and to prevent erosion

Chapter 21

Metal in body can cause serious damage to brain, kidneys, nervous system; used extensively in paint; must be discussed when selling a house built before 1978

Chapter 21

Colorless, odorless poisonous gas produced as a by-product of incomplete combustion; can be dangerous if not properly ventilated

Chapter 21

Radioactive odorless, tasteless gas; with long-term exposure can cause lung cancer

Chapter 21

Passed in 1980, established Superfund to clean up uncontrolled hazardous waste sites and to respond to spills

Chapter 21

Often used to store petroleum, if leaking can contaminate groundwater; only 10% of tank needs to be underground to require monitoring

Chapter 21

Generated by movement of electrical currents; prolonged exposure may cause cancer; major concern for property owners near high-voltage lines

Chapter 21

Gases that leak out of UFFI become trapped in building, may cause respiratory problems

Chapter 21

Sealing off of disintegrating asbestos or chipping and peeling lead-based paint; may be preferable to removal; still leaves hazard behind

Chapter 21

Multiple Choice (Continued)

4. T F Radon is a naturally occurring substance that is suspected of being a cause of lung cancer.

5. T F Urea-formaldehyde foam insulation has been proven harmful to humans.

6. T F The movement of electricity through high-tension power lines, secondary distribution lines, electrical transformers and clock radios creates electromagnetic fields.

7. T F Groundwater is water that lies on the earth's surface.

8. T F Underground storage tanks involved in the collection of storm water or wastewater are exempt from federal regulations.

9. T F The process of laying two to four feet of soil over the top of a landfill site and then planting foliage to prevent erosion is referred to as "layering."

10. T F Liability under Superfund is strict, joint and several, and retroactive.

Multiple Choice

Circle A, B, C or D

1. Prior to 1978, asbestos was a component of more than 3,000 types of building materials and is currently present in what percentage of commercial and public buildings in the United States?
   A. 10 percent
   B. 12 percent
   C. 20 percent
   D. 33 percent

2. Lead is commonly found in all of the following, EXCEPT
   A. water pipes.
   B. alkyd oil-based paint.
   C. automobile exhaust.
   D. insulating material.

3. J accepts an offer from K on her vintage Victorian home, built in 1892. Based on these facts, all of the following statements are true, EXCEPT
   A. J must attach a lead-based paint disclosure statement to the sales contract.
   B. If J is aware of any lead-based paint on the premises, she must disclose that fact to K.
   C. If K requests a lead-based paint inspection, J has 10 days in which to obtain one at her own expense.
   D. K is entitled to receive a pamphlet that describes the hazards posed by lead-based paint.

4. Where in the United States does radon occur?
   A. Mostly in the western states
   B. Mostly in the warm southern and southwestern regions
   C. In every state the United States
   D. Only in large urban areas

5. All of the following have been proven to pose a health hazard, EXCEPT
   A. asbestos.
   B. electromagnetic fields.
   C. lead-based paint.
   D. radon.

6. H stores toxic chemical waste in a large steel tank that has only 15 percent of its volume underground. J lives far out in the wilderness and has her own gas pump connected to a 1,000-gallon tank of gasoline buried ten feet underground near her garage. L keeps three large tanks filled with formaldehyde and battery acid in his basement. Which of these people are NOT exempt from federal regulations regarding USTs?
   A. H, J and L
   B. J and L only
   C. L only
   D. H only

Multiple Choice (Continued)

7. Which of the following is responsible for administering Superfund?
   A. CERCLA
   B. PRP
   C. EPA
   D. HUD

8. Proof of all of the following is necessary for innocent landowner immunity, EXCEPT the
   A. pollution was caused by a third party.
   B. landowner exercised "due care" when the property was purchased.
   C. landowner is a lender who acquired the property as a result of foreclosure.
   D. landowner had no actual or constructive knowledge of the damage.

9. In 1972, the PKL Chemical Co. owned Graylake and used both the lake and surrounding woodland as a dumping ground for millions of gallons of toxic waste chemicals. In 1979, PKL sold the property to D, its vice president, who built the Graylake Office Park. In 1990, D sold the development to H, who tore down the offices and built the Waterland Fun Park. H borrowed half of the $500,000 purchase price from Big Bank.

   In 1996, the EPA informed H that the Fun Park was built on a toxic dump and that the lake was a bubbling stew of deadly chemicals. Cleanup costs would be nearly $1 billion. Based on these facts, who is responsible for clean up under SARA?
   A. PKL, D and H only; lenders are immune under SARA.
   B. H only; retroactivity does not apply under these facts.
   C. PKL, D, H and Big Bank are jointly, severally and retroactively liable, although H and Big Bank may have innocent landowner immunity.
   D. PKL, D, H and Big Bank are jointly, severally and retroactively liable, and the strict liability imposed by CERCLA prohibits any immunities under SARA.

10. If a PRP refuses to pay the expenses of cleaning up a toxic site, the EPA may
    A. bring a criminal action and have the PRP jailed for up to ten years.
    B. bring a civil action and be awarded three times the actual cost of the cleanup.
    C. bring an administrative action and be awarded the actual cost of the cleanup, plus court costs.
    D. may have no legal recourse.

11. Sealing asbestos instead of removing it is called
    A. encapsulation.
    B. capping.
    C. irresponsible.
    D. extended liability.

12. The Lead-Based Paint Hazard Reduction Act applies to homes built before
    A. 1974.
    B. 1978.
    C. 1996.
    D. 1999.

13. All of the following can affect the radon levels in a home EXCEPT
    A. age of the home.
    B. weather conditions.
    C. soil density under the house.
    D. time of the year.

14. Identify the by-product of fuel combustion that may result in death in poorly ventilated areas.
    A. Radon
    B. Lead
    C. Urea Formaldehyde Foam Insulation
    D. Carbon monoxide

15. A storage tank is partially buried. How much of the tank must be underground to be considered an underground storage tank?
    A. 10 percent
    B. 15 percent
    C. 25 percent
    D. 35 percent

Answer Key

MATCHING

1. asbestos
2. encapsulation
3. lead
4. radon
5. urea formaldehyde
6. electromagnetic field
7. water table
8. landfill
9. capping
10. Superfund

Answer Key (Continued)

TRUE OR FALSE

1. False The Environmental Protection Agency estimates that approximately 20 percent of commercial and public buildings built prior to 1978 contain asbestos insulation.
2. False Asbestos removal is a dangerous, expensive process that can be performed only by trained and licensed technicians under controlled conditions.
3. False Under the 1996 regulations published by the Environmental Protection Agency and the Department of Housing and Urban Development, owners of homes built prior to 1978 are not required to test their properties for the presence of lead-based paint, but must fill out a lead-based paint disclosure statement.
4. True
5. True
6. True
7. False Groundwater is water that lies under the earth's surface.
8. True
9. False The process of laying two to four feet of soil over the top of a landfill site and then planting foliage to prevent erosion is referred to as "capping."
10. True

MULTIPLE CHOICE

1. C One out of five buildings may contain asbestos.
2. D Asbestos is the former insulating material, not lead.
3. C No one is required to test for lead, but the federal law gives the prospective buyer ten days (or any time agreed to or the buyer may waive the right) to have the home tested for lead at the buyer's expense.
4. C Radon has been found in every state, although some states are more likely than others. The only way to know for sure is to have the home tested.
5. B Most electrical appliances create a small or greater field of EMFs, but there is much conflicting advice about whether EMFs pose a health hazard.
6. D H's tank is more than 10 percent underground so his storage of toxic chemical waste should be monitored. J's tank is less than the 1,100 gallons so it is exempt, and since L's tanks are in his basement, but not underground, he is also exempt.
7. C CERCLA is administered and monitored by the EPA.
8. C Even landowners who were not responsible for the contamination have had to pay to clean it up; so have many lenders who foreclosed on a property only to find out that it was contaminated and the lender had to clean it up.
9. C Not only the present owner, but all of the owners in the past may be held responsible for the cleanup. Innocent landowner immunity may apply to H and to Big Bank.
10. B A PRP is a potentially responsible party. If the PRP does not clean up the site, the EPA will and then bills the PRP for the cost. Then, if the PRP still refuses to pay, the EPA can seek damages in court for up to three times the actual cost of cleanup.
11. A Capping is covering over the top of a landfill with dirt and landscaping.
12. B Target housing under LBPHRA is 1978 as that is the year that lead was banned from most paints.
13. A The age of the home is not a determining factor as to radon levels in the home. How many fans and how airtight it is would be of more concern.
14. D Carbon monoxide is the colorless, odorless and tasteless gas that is a by-product of incomplete combustion. High concentrations can lead to death.
15. A The official definition of an underground storage tank is at least 10 percent is underground.

22

Closing the Real Estate Transaction

Matching

Write the matching term on the appropriate line.

- accrued items
- federally related loans
- banking year
- closing
- credit
- debit
- escrow
- kickback
- prepaid items
- proration

1. ______________ The consummation of a real estate transaction
2. ______________ A method of closing in which a disinterested third party acts as the agent of both buyer and seller to coordinate the closing activities
3. ______________ The type of loan governed by RESPA
4. ______________ A charge that a party owes and must pay at closing
5. ______________ An amount that has already been paid, that is being reimbursed or that will be paid in the future
6. ______________ The division of financial responsibility for various items between the buyer and seller
7. ______________ Charges owed by the seller that will be paid by the buyer
8. ______________ Charges that have been paid by and are credited to the seller
9. ______________ A 360-day period used in calculating prorations
10. ______________ An unearned fee, paid as part of a real estate transaction, that is prohibited by RESPA

True or False

Circle the answer

1. T F At closing, the seller receives the purchase price and the buyer receives the property.
2. T F Shortly before the closing takes place, the buyer will usually conduct a final inspection of the property, usually called a "spot survey."
3. T F While the particulars of closing in escrow vary from state to state, the escrow agent is always a licensed attorney.
4. T F When closing in escrow, the seller will deposit proof of hazard insurance with the escrow agent.
5. T F Property sellers no longer have to buy a more expensive home to avoid paying a capital gains tax.
6. T F RESPA applies to all federally related loans, except for those administered by HUD.

Flash Cards (Pull out page & cut with scissors)

affidavit of title	good faith estimate (GFE)
closing statement	kickbacks
computerized loan origination	prepaid item
controlled business arrangement	proration
credit, debit	Real Estate Settlement Procedures Act (RESPA)
escrow	Uniform Settlement Statement (HUD-1)

Settlement costs that borrower is likely to incur; must be given within three business days after loan application; should be pretty accurate

Chapter 22

Written statement, made under oath, that grantor identifies himself and marital status, certifies that there are no new defects on title

Chapter 22

Prohibited unearned fees when no service has been rendered; i.e., receiving fees for making referrals to lenders, attorneys, surveyors, appraisers, etc.

Chapter 22

Detailed cash accounting of a real estate transaction showing all cash received, all charges and credits made and all cash paid out in the transaction

Chapter 22

On closing statement, items that have been paid by the seller, such as real estate taxes, for which he or she must be reimbursed by the buyer (credit seller, debit buyer)

Chapter 22

Electronic network for handling loan applications through remote computer terminals linked to various lenders' computers; borrower must pay for this extra service

Chapter 22

Expenses, either prepaid or paid in arrears, that are divided or distributed between buyer and seller at closing

Chapter 22

One-stop shopping for real estate consumers; consumer must be informed of relationship among the service providers and that others are available

Chapter 22

Federal law that requires certain disclosures to consumers about mortgage loan settlements; prohibits paying or receiving kickbacks and certain kinds of referral fees

Chapter 22

On closing statement, amount entered in a person's favor; either an amount that party has paid or amount for which party must be reimbursed; debit is amount charged

Chapter 22

Form required by RESPA includes all charges that will be collected at closing, whether required by the lender or a third party; must be available day before closing

Chapter 22

Closing of transaction through third party called escrow agent; who receives funds and documents to be delivered upon performance of certain instructions

Chapter 22

Multiple Choice (Continued)

7. T F Real estate licensees are exempt from RESPA's rules governing controlled business arrangements and referrals.

8. T F A special HUD information booklet must be provided to all real estate loan applicants.

9. T F Borrowers have the right to inspect the completed HUD-1 form one day prior to closing.

10. T F RESPA's rules prohibit both paying and receiving a kickback.

Multiple Choice

Circle A, B, C or D

For Questions 1 through 4, prorate using a 30-day month and a 360-day year; prorate the taxes as of the close of escrow. Split the escrow fee 50-50 between the parties. Use the following relevant facts:

- ♦ Purchase price: $25,000 cash
- ♦ Earnest money: $1,000
- ♦ Commission rate: 7 percent
- ♦ Revenue stamps: $25
- ♦ Real estate taxes: $350 (paid in full for current year)
- ♦ Title insurance : $153.51
- ♦ Recording fee: $2
- ♦ Escrow fee: $168
- ♦ Loan balance: $9,450, (existing mortgage including credit for the reserve account)

1. What amount is the buyer debited for the real estate taxes?
   A. $145.83
   B. $146.71
   C. $202.19
   D. $203.30

2. What amount is the seller debited for the broker's commission?
   A. $750
   B. $1,650
   C. $1,750
   D. $2,500

3. What amount of the escrow fee will the buyer pay?
   A. $56
   B. $84
   C. $160
   D. $168

4. What is the real estate commission in this transaction?
   A. $1,750
   B. $1,754
   C. $1,780
   D. $1,790

5. A sale is closing on August 31. Real estate taxes, calculated on a calendar year basis, have not been paid for the current year. The tax is estimated to be $1,800. What amount of proration will be credited to the buyer?
   A. $1,100
   B. $1,200
   C. $1,485
   D. $1,500

6. A seller would be responsible for providing all of the following items, EXCEPT
   A. evidence of title.
   B. affidavits of title.
   C. the deed.
   D. documentation for a new loan.

7. How long must a lender retain a HUD-1 after the date of closing?
   A. Six months
   B. One year
   C. Two years
   D. Four years

8. L owns a fully occupied rental apartment building. If L sells the apartment building to K, how will the tenant's security deposits be reflected on the closing statement?
   A. Credit L, debit K
   B. Debit both L and K
   C. Credit K, debit L
   D. Security deposits are not reflected on a closing statement.

Multiple Choice (Continued)

9. Q is purchasing 345 Minor Street from G. The single-family home is subject to an existing 30-year mortgage of $86,500 at a fixed rate of 6 percent. Under the terms of the sales contract, Q will assume G's mortgage at 6 percent interest and pay the federally insured lender's standard assumption fee of $75. In addition, G will assist Q by taking back a purchase-money mortgage in the amount of $25,000 at 8 percent interest. Is this transaction subject to RESPA?
   A. No, because this transaction involves a purchase-money mortgage taken back by the seller.
   B. No, because the terms of the assumed loan are modified and the lender's fee exceeds $50.
   C. Yes, because the seller is taking back a purchase-money mortgage at an interest rate higher than that charged for the assumed loan.
   D. Yes, because the terms of the assumed loan are modified and the lender's fee exceeds $50.

10. Since 1972, M, a real estate broker, has had an understanding with two of the five mortgage lenders in town. M recommends only those two lenders to her clients and does not tell clients about any other lenders. In return, the recommended lenders pay for the vacations M offers her salespeople as rewards for high performance. Based on these facts, which of the following statements is true?
    A. M is not doing anything illegal.
    B. Because this arrangement has been in existence for more than 15 years, it is exempt from RESPA.
    C. This is a permissible controlled business arrangement under RESPA, because M is not paid a fee for the recommendations.
    D. M's arrangement with the lenders is an illegal kickback under RESPA.

Continued on page 182

Closing Statement

Fill in the form

Complete the settlement statement worksheet shown in Figure 22.1 on the opposite page, based on the information provided below. Carry out all computations to three decimal places until the final calculation. Prorate based on a 30-day month. The buyer's and seller's statements should be viewed separately, although many items will appear on both. Although both the buyer's and the seller's total debits and credits must balance, their totals and cash due need not. Selling price for the property is $115,000; the earnest money deposit is $12,000.

♦ Buyers:	Doug & Connie Cornwall	♦ Loan origination:	$2,460 fee (3 points); paid by buyer
♦ Seller:	Cordelia Lear	♦ Transfer tax:	$.50 per $500; paid by seller
♦ Property address:	1604 North Albany	♦ Recording fees:	$10.00 per document (deed and new mortgage paid by buyer; release of mortgage paid by seller)
♦ Closing date:	June 30 of the current year	♦ Attorney's fees:	$300 buyer; $450 seller
♦ Broker's fee:	7 percent commission	♦ Title insurance:	owner's policy $700 (seller); mortgagee's policy $150 (buyer)
♦ Property taxes:	$1,750/year; this year's taxes have not yet been paid	♦ Document prep:	$50; paid by buyer
♦ Loan Payoff:	$43,000 balance of principal and accrued interest	♦ Survey: $150;	paid by seller
♦ Financing:	buyer is obtaining a new $82,000 first mortgage loan		

CLOSING STATEMENT

PROPERTY: ______________________________

SELLER(S): ______________________________

BUYER(S): ______________________________

SETTLEMENT DATE: ______________

	BUYER		SELLER	
SETTLEMENT ITEM	**DEBIT**	**CREDIT**	**DEBIT**	**CREDIT**
Purchase Price				
TOTALS				
Due From BUYER				
Due So SELLER				

Figure 22.1

Multiple Choice (Continued)

For questions 12 through 14, prorate using the actual number of days in the month and year. Split the escrow fee 50-50. The purchaser assumes the existing mortgage balance of $127,042.42; the purchaser will pay cash at the closing in the amount of the difference between the purchase price and the loan balance; the present monthly payment on the loan is $1,101.40. Closing is October 15. Other facts:

- ♦ Purchase price: $350,000
- ♦ Earnest money: $3,500
- ♦ Commission rate: 6 percent split 50-50
- ♦ Real estate taxes: $2,900 (paid in full for the current year)
- ♦ Escrow fee: $800
- ♦ Title insurance: $1,150
- ♦ Insurance policy: $758 (annual premium)
- ♦ Revenue stamps: $126.30
- ♦ Recording fee: $30
- ♦ Interest rate: 8.75 (percent, with the next payment due November 1)

11. All of the following items are usually prorated at closing, EXCEPT
    A. prepaid general real estate taxes.
    B. interest on an assumed loan.
    C. appraisal fees.
    D. rents.

12. What are the prorated real estate taxes to be charged to the buyer?
    A. $604.20 C. $690.67
    B. $611.77 D. $728.30

13. What will be the amount of commission paid to the cooperating broker?
    A. $8,750 C. $17,500
    B. $10,500 D. $21,000

14. What amount will the seller receive at the closing?
    A. $201,548.19 C. $217,749.28
    B. $205,572.33 D. $208,654.34

15. How is earnest money treated if the buyer does not default and shows up for closing?
    A. Credit seller C. Credit buyer
    B. Debit buyer D. Debit seller

Answer Key

MATCHING

1. closing
2. escrow
3. federally related loans
4. debit
5. credit
6. proration
7. accrued items
8. prepaid items
9. banking year
10. kickback

TRUE OR FALSE

1. True

2. False Shortly before the closing takes place, the buyer will usually conduct a final inspection of the property, usually called a " walk through."

3. False While the particulars of closing in escrow vary from state to state, the escrow agent may be an attorney, title company, trust company, escrow company or a lender's escrow department.

4. False When closing in escrow, the buyer will deposit proof of hazard insurance with the escrow agent.

5. True

6. False RESPA applies to all federally related loans, including those administered by HUD.

Answer Key (Continued)

7. False Real estate licensees are not exempt from RESPA's rules governing controlled business arrangements and referrals.

8. True

9. True

10. True

MULTIPLE CHOICE

1. A $350 ÷ 12 x 5 = $145.83

2. C $25,000 x 7% = $1,750

3. B $168 ÷ 2 = $84

4. A $25,000 x 7% = $1,750

5. B $1,800 ÷ 12 x 8 = $1,200

6. D Documentation for the new loan is the responsibility of the buyer.

7. C One should retain the HUD-1 for at least two years

8. C L must pay the security deposit to K who will, as the new owner, be responsible for returning the money to the tenant at the end of the lease.

9. D It would not have been had the loan not been modified and if the assumption had been less than $50.

10. D By not telling her clients about the other lenders in town, M is limiting their ability to get the best possible financing. That added to the fact that the lender pays for her salespeople's vacations look very suspicious.

11. C Usually, the lender asks that the appraisal fees and credit report fees be paid outside of closing (POC).

12. A $2,900 ÷ 365 x 76 = $604.20

    The seller pays taxes on the day of closing. There are 15 days left in October, 30 in November, and 31 in December. Thus, the buyer owes the seller for 76 days

13. B $350,000 x 6% ÷ 2 = $10,500

14. A $350,000 - $21,000 + $604.20 - $400 + $127,042.42 -$126.30 - $487.29 = $201,548.19 (The seller owes accrued interest on the loan for the 16 days he used the money: $127,042.42 x 8.75% ÷ 365 x 16 = $487.29)

15. C The earnest money is brought to closing and credited to the buyer.

Answer Key (Continued)

CLOSING STATEMENT

PROPERTY: ______________________

SELLER(S): ______________________

BUYER(S): ______________________

SETTLEMENT DATE: ______________

	BUYER		SELLER	
SETTLEMENT ITEM	DEBIT	CREDIT	DEBIT	CREDIT
Purchase Price	115,000	--	--	115,000
Earnest Money	--	12,000	--	--
Broker's Commision	--	--	8,050	--
Property Taxes	--	875	875	--
Payoff Existing Mortgage	--	--	43,000	--
New First Mortgage	--	82,000	--	--
Loan Origination Fee	2,460	--	--	--
Transfer Tax	--	--	115	--
Recording Fees	20	--	10	--
Attorney's Fees	300	--	450	--
Title Insurance	150	--	700	--
Document Preparation	50	--	--	--
Survey	--	--	150	--
TOTALS	117,980	94,875	53,350	115,000
Due from BUYER	--	23,105	--	--
Due to SELLER	--	--	61,650	--
	117,980	117,980	115,000	115,000